Paths to College and Career

English Language Arts

Understanding Perspectives

PCG | *Education*

JB JOSSEY-BASS™
A Wiley Brand

CONTENTS

Unit 2   89

Unit 3   **197**

Notice/Wonder Note-Catcher

Name: _____

Date: _____

Notice	Wonder
Preface, *Unbroken*	
Gallery Walk	

Partner Discussion Starters

I hear that you said . . .

I'm still wondering . . .

Now that I know that, I think . . .

What you said about . . . raised a question for me. (Ask question.)

Gallery Walk Photograph

7th War Loan

Source: Cecil Calvert Beall, "7th War Loan. Now—All Together" (1945), Prints and Photographs Division, Library of Congress, Washington, D.C. http://www.loc.gov/pictures/item/95501013/.

Boy on Suitcase

Source: Russell Lee, "Los Angeles, California. Japanese-American Child Who Is Being Evacuated with His Parents to Owens Valley" (1942), Prints and Photographs Division, Library of Congress, Washington, D.C. http://www.loc.gov/pictures/item/fsa1998003572/PP/.

USS *Neosho,* Navy Oil Tanker, Leaving Berth, Surrounded by Stricken Ships, in Order to Escape Japanese Attack

Source: Official United States Navy photograph (Dec. 7, 1941). http://www.loc.gov/pictures/item/owi2002048491/PP/.

USS *Arizona,* at Height of Fire, Following Japanese Aerial Attack on Pearl Harbor, Hawaii

Source: United States Navy, "USS Arizona, at Height of Fire, Following Japanese Aerial Attack on Pearl Harbor, Hawaii" (Dec. 7, 1941), Prints and Photographs Division. Library of Congress, Washington, D.C. http://www.loc.gov/pictures/item/92500933/.

Major General M. F. Harmon, Commanding the United States Army in the South Pacific Area, Pointing to His Map as Two Members of His Staff Look On

Source: Farm Security Administration, Office of War Information, "Major General M. F. Harmon, commanding the United States Army in the South Pacific area, pointing to his map as two members of his staff, Brigadier General N. F. Twining, chief of staff, and Colonel G. C. Jamieson, look on. The picture was taken in front of the headquarters in New Caledonia" (1942), Overseas Picture Division, Library of Congress, Washington, D.C. http://www.loc.gov/pictures/collection/fsa/item/owi2001045256/PP/.

"The Walkers Club," Eight U.S. Airmen in China Who Were Forced Down Behind the Japanese Lines

Source: Farm Security Administration, Office of War Information, "The Walkers Club" (between 1940 and 1946), Overseas Picture Division, Library of Congress, Washington, D.C. http://www.loc.gov/pictures/item/oem2002008628/PP/.

Manzanar Street Scene, Winter, Manzanar Relocation Center

Source: Ansel Adams, "Manzanar Street Scene, Winter, Manzanar Relocation Center" (1943), Prints and Photographs Division, Library of Congress, Washington, D.C. http://www.loc.gov/pictures/item/2002695965/.

Entrance to Manzanar, Manzanar Relocation Center

Source: Ansel Adams, "Entrance to Manzanar, Manzanar Relocation Center" (1943), Prints and Photographs Division, Library of Congress, Washington, D.C. http://www.loc.gov/pictures/collection/manz/item/2002695960/.

Unbroken Structured Notes

Preface, Pages 3–6

Name: _____

Date: _____

What's the gist of what you read in the preface and pages 3–6?

Focus Question

Use details from the text to describe Louie's character as shown in pages 3–6. What aspects of his character that you have read about so far may help him survive the situation described in the preface?

Vocabulary

Word	Definition	Context clues: How did you figure out this word?
loped (3)		
transfixed (4)		
corralled (5)		
untamable (6)		
insurgency (6)		

Vocabulary Square

Name: _____

Date: _____

Definition in your own words	Synonym or variations
Part of speech and prefix/suffix/root (as applicable)	**Sketch or symbol**

Discussion Appointments

Pacific Theater Partners

Name: _____

Date: _____

Make one appointment at each location.

Pearl Harbor	
Midway	
Marshall Islands	
Iwo Jima	
Okinawa	

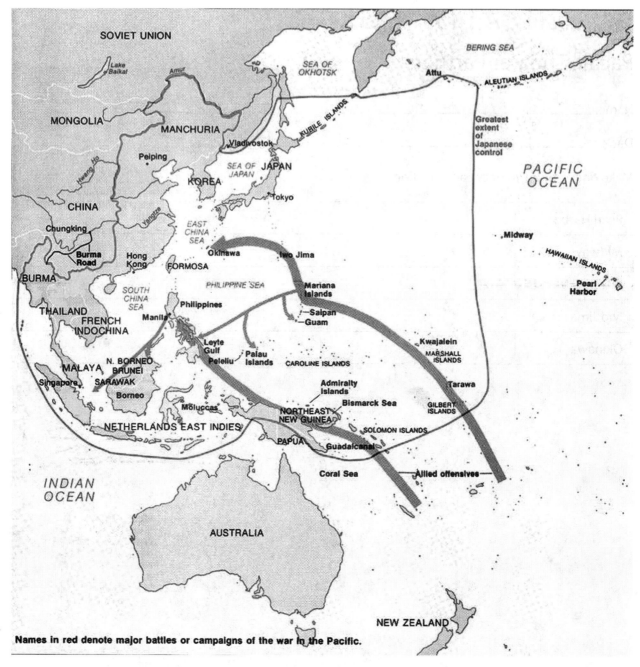

Names in red denote major battles or campaigns of the war in the Pacific.

Source: "Map of the Pacific Theatre 1941–1945." Online image, Perry-Castañeda Library Map Collection, University of Texas Libraries. http://www.lib.utexas.edu/maps/national_parks/pacific_theater_1941_45.jpg.

Quick Write

Allusions

Name: **Nyla Winters**

Date: **Thu mar 4**

On page 4, Hillenbrand writes, "The ship passed over Nuremberg, where fringe politician Adolf Hitler, whose Nazi Party had been trounced in the 1928 election, had just delivered a speech touting selective infanticide. Then it flew east of Frankfurt, where a Jewish woman named Edith Frank was caring for her newborn, a girl named Anne." Why do you think Hillenbrand uses these *allusions*, references to Adolf Hitler and Anne Frank, as part of Louie's story?

_____

_____

_____

_____

_____

_____

_____

_____

_____

_____

_____

_____

_____

_____

_____

_____

_____

Unbroken Structured Notes

Pages 6–12

Name: _____

Date: _____

What's the gist of what you read on pages 6–12?

Focus Question

On page 7, Hillenbrand writes, "When history carried him into war, this resilient optimism would define him." How is Louie resilient and optimistic? What does it mean to "define him"? Use the strongest evidence from the book to support your answer.

EXPEDITIONARY
LEARNING

Vocabulary

Word	Definition	Context clues: How did you figure out this word?
skulked (6)		
magnum opus (7)		
resilient (7)		
optimism (7)		
surreptitious (10)		
eugenics (11)		

Frayer Model

Resilient

Name: _____

Date: _____

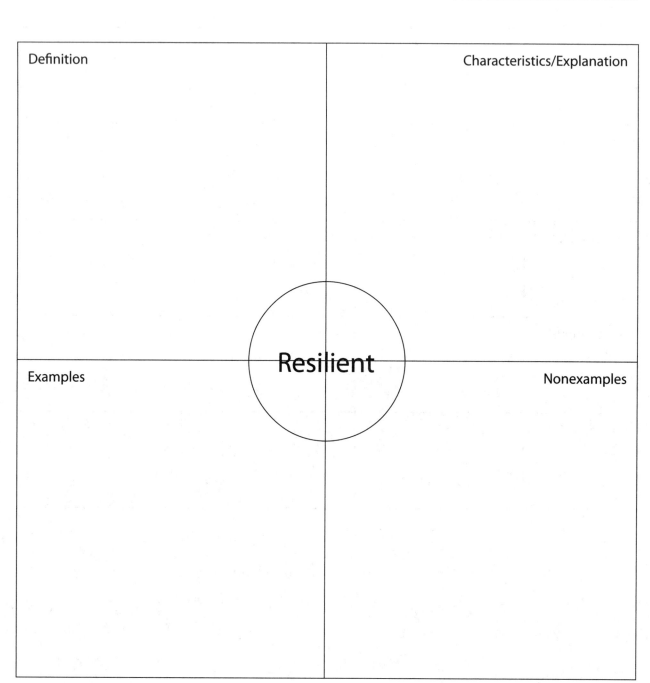

Definition	Characteristics/Explanation

Resilient

Examples	Nonexamples

Text-Dependent Questions

Louie's Change of Heart

Name: _____

Date: _____

Text-dependent questions	Response using the strongest evidence from the text
1. What motivates Louie to attempt to change his ways?	
2. How does trying to change work out for him?	
3. How does Louie demonstrate self-examination or reflection?	
4. How does his line of thinking change in this passage?	

Unbroken Structured Notes

Pages 13–18

Name: _____

Date: _____

What's the gist of what you read on pages 13–18?

Focus Question

Hillenbrand refers to the change in Louie as "rehabilitation" (13). How is Louie rehabilitated? Use the strongest evidence from the text to support your answer.

Vocabulary

Word	Definition	Context clues: How did you figure out this word?
rehabilitation (13)		
incipient (14)		
restiveness (16)		
obliterating (16)		
biomechanical (17)		

"War in the Pacific"

Source: "World War II: Americans in the Pacific," *Cobblestone: The Magazine for Young People* 15, no. 1 (Jan. 1994). Copyright © 1994 by Carus Publishing Company. Cobblestone Publishing, 30 Grove Street, Suite C, Peterborough, NH 03458. All rights reserved. Used by permission of the publisher. www.cobblestonepub.com.

Name: _____

Date: _____

Text		Vocabulary Words and Definitions
1	THE BIG PICTURE In 1854, a U.S. naval squadron led by Commodore Matthew Perry arrived in Tokyo Bay, near the Japanese capital. For more than two centuries, Japan had avoided almost all contact with Europeans and Americans. Perry's visit helped reopen Japan to foreign trade, and the Japanese began to adopt European technology (such as steamships, railroads, and modern weapons) and many European-style institutions (schools, a national legislature, and an army and navy).	
2	The Japanese also adopted the policy of imperialism, or colonialism. Many Japanese believed that if Japan was to become wealthy and powerful, it needed to acquire industrially important colonies. In 1894, Japan went to war with China and a year later won Korea and the island of Formosa (now Taiwan). Over the next four decades, Japan seized territory in Asia and the Pacific from China, Russia, and Germany.	
3	By 1937, military leaders controlled Japan. In July, the Japanese launched an all-out war to take over China. The Japanese conquered much of eastern China, but by 1939, the two countries had fought to a stalemate. The United States sided with China against Japan, but most Americans did not want to go to war so far from home. Still, President Franklin D. Roosevelt threatened to cut American trade with Japan if it did not withdraw from China. In May 1940, he stationed the U.S. Pacific Fleet at Pearl Harbor, Hawaii, as a further warning to Japan.	

4	But the Japanese did not stop. By August 1940, Japanese troops occupied the northern part of French Indochina (now Vietnam). In September, Japan signed a treaty of cooperation with Germany and Italy, whose armies were busy **overrunning**[1] Europe and North Africa. In July 1941, the Japanese occupied the southern part of Indochina. Roosevelt, busy aiding Britain in its war against Germany, ordered a freeze on trade with Japan.	
5	Japan had little oil of its own; without oil and gasoline from the United States, its army and navy could not fight. In October 1941, a new Japanese government, led by General Hideki Tojo, faced a dilemma. If Japan withdrew from China, American trade would resume, but the proud Japanese army would be humiliated. If the Japanese remained in China, Japan would need a new source of oil.	
6	Tojo and his advisors knew that the United States would have a big advantage over Japan in a long **campaign**.[2] The United States had more people, money, and factories to manufacture weapons and war supplies. But the Japanese believed that the Americans and British, already deeply involved in the war against Germany, did not have the military strength to defend their Asian and Pacific territories. The Japanese had a large, modern navy and an army hardened by years of combat in China. They hoped that many quick victories over the Americans and British would force peace, leaving Japan in control of eastern Asia and the western Pacific.	

7	As the Japanese prepared for war, the Tojo government continued negotiating with the United States, hoping that Roosevelt might change his mind and resume trade with Japan. But the United States demanded that Japan withdraw from both Indochina and China. Roosevelt was confident that the Japanese would not risk attacking the powerful United States.	
8	As negotiations continued in the fall of 1941, the U.S. Army and Navy rushed to reinforce Hawaii and the Philippine Islands. U.S. military leaders warned Roosevelt that their forces would not be ready for war until the spring of 1942.	
9	On December 1, 1941, Tojo's government, with the consent of Japan's emperor, Hirohito, decided to end negotiations and attack U.S. forces on December 8 (December 7 in the United States). For strategic reasons, the Japanese planned a lightning strike on the huge naval force at Pearl Harbor. American leaders knew that Japan was about to strike (U.S. intelligence officials had broken the Japanese diplomatic code), but they did not know that Pearl Harbor would be a target.	

[1]Overrunning: invading
[2]Campaign: a series of military actions

Map of the Pacific

East Asia and Oceania

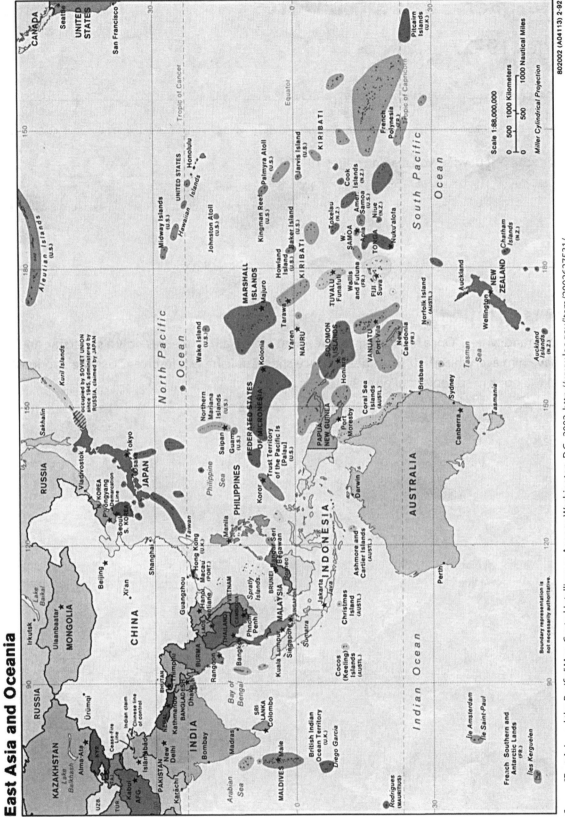

Source: "East Asia and the Pacific." Map. Central Intelligence Agency, Washington, D.C., 2002. http://www.loc.gov/item/2002627531/.

Unbroken Structured Notes

Pages 19–27

Name: _____

Date: _____

What's the gist of what you read on pages 19–27?

Focus Question

Hillenbrand writes, "Once his hometown's resident archvillain, Louie was now a superstar, and Torrance forgave him everything" (20). How did Torrance show Louie he was forgiven? Use the strongest evidence from the book to support your answer.

EXPEDITIONARY
LEARNING

Vocabulary

Word	Definition	Context clues: How did you figure out this word?
disillusioned (19)		
touted (19)		
routed (19)		
prodigy (21)		
barn burner (22)		

Understanding Perspectives

Pearl Harbor Graphic Organizer

Name: _____

Date: _____

	Year	Action	Did this escalate the conflict between the United States and Japan? Explain.
Japanese actions BEFORE the Pearl Harbor attack			

	Year	Action	Did this escalate the conflict between the United States and Japan? Explain.
U.S. actions BEFORE the Pearl Harbor attack			

Unbroken Structured Notes

Pages 28–37

Name: _____

Date: _____

What's the gist of what you read on pages 28–37?

Focus Question

What do Louie's antics in Germany reveal about his character and values? Use the strongest evidence from the book to support your answer.

Vocabulary

Word	Definition	Context clues: How did you figure out this word?
plundering (28)		
coltish (28)		
prodigious (31)		
surreal (32)		
penultimate (34)		

"Day of Infamy" Speech

Given by President Franklin Delano Roosevelt
December 8, 1941

Source: President Franklin D. Roosevelt to Congress, "Transcript of Joint Address to Congress Leading to a Declaration of War Against Japan," Dec. 8, 1941. Library of Congress, Washington, D.C. Public domain.

Name: _____

Date: _____

What's the gist of this section?	Mr. Vice President, Mr. Speaker, Members of the Senate, and of the House of Representatives: Yesterday, December 7th, 1941—a date which will live in infamy—the United States of America was suddenly and deliberately attacked by naval and air forces of the Empire of Japan. The United States was at peace with that nation and, at the solicitation of Japan, was still in conversation with its government and its emperor looking toward the maintenance of peace in the Pacific.
	infamy: evil fame *solicitation: request* *maintenance: to work to keep something the way it is*
	1. According to this document, what was the relationship like between the United States and Japan before the attack on Pearl Harbor?

What's the gist of this section?	Indeed, one hour after Japanese air squadrons had commenced bombing in the American island of Oahu, the Japanese ambassador to the United States and his colleague delivered to our Secretary of State a formal reply to a recent American message. And while this reply stated that it seemed useless to continue the existing **diplomatic negotiations**, it contained no threat or hint of war or of armed attack.
	diplomatic negotiations: when two or more countries have discussions in order to reach an agreement *Paraphrase: An hour after the Japanese started bombing in Oahu, the Japanese ambassador delivered a reply to an earlier message that stated that the Japanese and the United States should not continue to negotiate with each other, but it did not mention a threat of war.*
What's the gist of this section?	It will be recorded that the distance of Hawaii from Japan makes it obvious that the attack was deliberately planned many days or even weeks ago. During the intervening time, the Japanese government has deliberately sought to deceive the United States by false statements and expressions of hope for continued peace.
	2. Roosevelt accuses the Japanese of seeking to deceive the United States. According to this speech, what is one example of an action in which the Japanese government deceived the United States?

What's the gist of this section?	The attack yesterday on the Hawaiian islands has caused severe damage to American naval and military forces. I regret to tell you that very many American lives have been lost. In addition, American ships have been reported torpedoed on the high seas between San Francisco and Honolulu.
	Yesterday, the Japanese government also launched an attack against Malaya.
	Last night, Japanese forces attacked Hong Kong.
	Last night, Japanese forces attacked Guam.
	Last night, Japanese forces attacked the Philippine Islands.
	Last night, the Japanese attacked Wake Island.
	And this morning, the Japanese attacked Midway Island.
	Japan has, therefore, undertaken a surprise offensive extending throughout the Pacific area. The facts of yesterday and today speak for themselves.
	3. At the time of this speech, the places mentioned here (Hawaii, Malaya, Hong Kong, Guam, Philippine Islands, Wake Island, and Midway Island) were controlled by either the United States or Great Britain. Why might Roosevelt list each one individually?

What's the gist of this section?	As commander in chief of the Army and Navy, I have directed that all measures be taken for our defense. But always will our whole nation remember the character of the onslaught against us.
	No matter how long it may take us to overcome this premeditated invasion, the American people in their righteous might will win through to absolute victory.
	I believe that I interpret the will of the Congress and of the people when I assert that we will not only defend ourselves to the uttermost, but will make it very certain that this form of treachery shall never again endanger us.
	will (n.): desire; want
	4. What does Roosevelt mean when he says the United States will "make it very certain that this form of treachery shall never again endanger us"?

What's the gist of this section?	Hostilities exist. There is no blinking at the fact that our people, our territory, and our interests are in grave danger.
	With confidence in our armed forces, with the unbounding determination of our people, we will gain the inevitable triumph—so help us God.
	I ask that the Congress declare that since the unprovoked and dastardly attack by Japan on Sunday, December 7th, 1941, a state of war has existed between the United States and the Japanese empire.
	grave (adj.): serious
	5. According to the last paragraph, what is the purpose of Roosevelt's speech?

Unbroken Structured Notes

Pages 38–47

Name: _____

Date: _____

What's the gist of what you read on pages 38–47?

Focus Question

Hillenbrand writes, "As Louie blazed through college, far away, history was turning"(43). Why does the author interrupt Louie's narrative with information about Japan and Germany? Use the strongest evidence from the book to support your answer.

Vocabulary

Word	Definition	Context clues: How did you figure out this word?
ardent (39)		
ruse (40)		
superlative (41)		
unmoored (44)		
bombardier (45)		

Close Reading Guide: War with Japan

Unbroken, Pages 38–47

Name: _____

Date: _____

Text-dependent questions	Respond using the strongest evidence from the text
1. Why does Hillenbrand include both the triumphs of Louie and the ominous background on Japan in the same chapter?	
2. What reasons does Hillenbrand give for Japan's plans to conquer new land?	
3. According to Hillenbrand, what belief was central to the Japanese identity?	
4. Hitler believed in the superiority of the Aryan (blond-haired, blue-eyed, German) race. How does this relate to the central Japanese belief described by Hillenbrand?	

5. What role does violence and brutality play in the Japanese identity, according to Hillenbrand?	
6. How did the situation with Germany affect Louie directly?	
7. Reread page 46 from "Not long after sunrise on a Sunday in December" to the end of that section, ending with "There were red circles on its wings" on page 47. List the strong descriptive details from this passage that Hillenbrand uses to describe the Pearl Harbor attack. Why does the author provide so much detail?	

EXPEDITIONARY
LEARNING

"Fourteen-Part Message"

Delivered by the Japanese Ambassador to the U.S. Secretary of State, December 7, 1941

Source: Japanese Note to the United States, December 7, 1941. Delivered as a telegram. *Department of State Bulletin* 5, no. 129 (Dec. 13, 1941). Public domain.

Name: _____

Date: _____

What's the gist of this section?	1. The government of Japan genuinely wants to come to a friendly understanding with the Government of the United States so that the two countries may secure peace in the Pacific Area and contribute toward world peace. Japan has continued sincere negotiations with the Government of the United States since last April. 2. The Japanese Government wants to insure the stability of East Asia and to promote world peace and thereby to enable each nation to find its proper place in the world.
	negotiation: resolving a conflict using compromise
	According to this document, what are three of the Japanese Government's goals?

What's the gist of this section?	Ever since Japan's war with China, the Japanese Government has tried to restore peace. However, the United States has resorted to every possible measure to assist China and to obstruct peace between Japan and China. Nevertheless, last August, the Premier of Japan proposed to meet the President of the United States for a discussion of important problems between the two countries. However, the American Government insisted that the meeting should take place after an agreement of view had been reached on fundamental and essential questions. *Paraphrase: The leader of Japan proposed a meeting with the president of the United States to discuss their problems in the Pacific, but the American government insisted that Japan and the U.S. agree on some things before the two leaders met.*
	obstruct: to block *fundamental and essential questions: the most important, basic questions or issues*
	According to this document, what are two ways the American government made it difficult for the Japanese Government to reach these goals?

What's the gist of this section?	3. Subsequently, on September 25th, the Japanese Government submitted a proposal, taking fully into consideration past American claims and also incorporating Japanese views. Repeated discussions did not help produce an agreement. The present cabinet, therefore, submitted a revised proposal, moderating still further the Japanese claims. But the American Government failed to display in the slightest degree a spirit of conciliation. The negotiation made no progress. *Paraphrase: Japan tried to suggest ideas for a compromise between itself and the United States, taking into account past conversations. The United States did not agree. Japan revised the compromise, but the American government would not compromise at all.*
	What does the document say is another way the American government made it difficult for the Japanese government to reach its goals?

What's the gist of this section?	Therefore, the Japanese Government, trying to avert a Japanese-American crisis, submitted still another proposal on November 20th, which included:
	(1) The Government of Japan and the United States will not **dispatch** armed forces into any of the regions, excepting French Indo-China, in the Southeastern Asia and the Southern Pacific area.
	(3) Both Governments will work to restore commercial relations. The Government of the United States shall supply Japan the required quantity of oil.
	The American Government, refusing to yield an inch, delayed the negotiation. It is difficult to understand this attitude of the American Government.
	Paraphrase: Japan then made another attempt at a compromise that included:
	• *Neither Japan nor the United States will send any armed forces to Southeast Asia or the southern Pacific.*
	• *The United States will stop its embargo of oil. (An embargo is when one country refuses to trade with another country.)*
	dispatch: send
	What two things did the Japanese Government ask for in its proposal?

What's the gist of this section?	The Japanese Government wants the American Government to know:
	1. The American Government **advocates**, in the name of world peace, ideas that are favorable to it. But the peace of the world may only be reached by discovering a **mutually** acceptable formula through recognition of the reality of the situation and mutual appreciation of one another's position. An attitude that ignores realities and imposes one's selfish views upon others will not **facilitate** successful negotiations.
	Paraphrase: The American government wants world peace, but only if it still gets what it wants. World peace will happen only through compromise. Making others accept one's selfish views will not help create agreements between countries.
	advocates: supports, argues for
	mutual: shared by both sides
	facilitate: enable, help with
	Diplomacy is the term used to describe when two or more countries discuss and negotiate to come to agreement. According to the Japanese government, what is U.S. diplomacy like?

What's the gist of this section?	3. The American Government objects to settling international issues through military pressure, but it uses **economic** pressure instead. Using economic pressure to deal with international relations should be **condemned**. It is, at times, more **inhumane** than military pressure.
	Paraphrase: The U.S. government says not to use military attacks and wars to end international conflicts. Instead, the U.S. government uses economic pressure, which means that it tries to control other countries by refusing to trade with them. This kind of economic pressure should not be used because it can be even more cruel than a military attack.
	economic: related to money or wealth
	condemn: to call or name something wrong
	inhumane: cruel
	Why do you think the authors of this message believe that using economic pressure against another country is worse than using military pressure?

What's the gist of this section?	4. It is impossible not to reach the conclusion that the American Government desires to maintain and strengthen its dominant position in East Asia. The Japanese Government cannot tolerate that, since it directly runs counter to Japan's fundamental policy to enable each nation to enjoy its proper place in the world. . . .
	7. Obviously the American Government's intention is to obstruct Japan's effort toward the establishment of peace through the creation of a new order in East Asia, and especially to preserve American interests by keeping Japan and China at war. This intention has been revealed clearly during the course of the present negotiation.
	Paraphrase: The only possible conclusion is that the United States wants to continue having a lot of control in East Asia because of the way the American government has handled these negotiations. The United States wants to keep Japan and China at war with each other.
	dominant: strongest, most powerful
	counter: against, opposite
	This document accuses the American government of interfering in Japan's relationship with China. Why does the Japanese government think the U.S. government is doing this? (In other words, what do they think America's goal is?)

What's the gist of this section?	Thus, the **earnest** hope of the Japanese Government to preserve the peace of the Pacific through cooperation with the American Government has finally been lost. The Japanese Government regrets to have to notify the American Government that it seems it is impossible to reach an agreement through further negotiations.
	earnest: honest and serious
	The Japanese government says that it seems "impossible to reach an agreement through further negotiations." Make an inference: What did the Japanese government do next?

Vocabulary Chart

Directions: Add words that are new to you from the reading. Do not add words that are defined for you already.

Word	Definition	Context clues: How did you figure out this word?

Sentence Starters

To paraphrase someone else's idea to make sure you understand, use:

> *I hear that you said . . .*

To ask a question or probe, use:

> *I'm wondering . . .*
>
> *I hear that you said . . . and I'm still wondering . . .*
>
> *Can you clarify what you meant when you said . . . ?*
>
> *What you said about . . . raised a question for me. My question is . . . ?*
>
> *It seems like what you said about . . . is different from what [someone else] said. (Name conflicting ideas)*

To show how something has changed your thinking, use:

> *Now that I know that, I need to change what I think about . . .*

To cite text evidence, use:

> *I hear that you said . . . , but I still think . . . because the text says . . . (Cite evidence)*
>
> *What you said about . . . reminded me of something I read in the text. (Cite evidence)*

Unbroken Structured Notes

Pages 51–60 and Summary of Pages 60–73

Name: _____

Date: _____

What is the gist of pages 51–60?

Summary of Pages 60–65

(Note: Refer to the diagram of the B-24 bomber on page 48 to better understand this section of the text.)

Louie and his crewmates are assigned to fly in a B-24 Liberator plane. They spend three months learning how to fly it and use its weapons to attack targets. Louie's job is to drop bombs on targets from the "greenhouse" (labeled "bombardier" on the diagram on page 48).

During training, Louie and the rest of the crew learn about the dangers of flying. They have radio trouble and get lost for three-and-a-half hours one night. Several other men they knew died in plane crashes. These kinds of accidents became so common that the Air Force started training men to "ditch" (land on water), jump out of planes safely, and survive after a crash.

Louie's plane has its share of problems: a fuel leak, broken gas gauges that sometimes say the plane is full of fuel when it is almost empty, and one engine that is "thirstier" for gas than the other one. Even though they know how dangerous their job is, Louie and the other men grow to love their plane and decide to name it *Super Man*. (See a picture of *Super Man* on page 64.)

On November 2, 1942, Louie and the rest of the crew of *Super Man* take off for Hawaii and their first mission of the war.

Summary of Pages 66–73

Louie and the rest of the *Super Man* crew arrive in Hawaii and move into the Kahuku barracks. They are ready to fight: "Everyone was eager to take a crack at the enemy, but there was no combat to be had" (67). The crew continues training, flying over Hawaii to practice bombing targets, but they often are bored and play practical jokes to keep themselves entertained.

On their days off, the men go to the movies and out to eat. Louie runs around the runway to stay in shape for the Olympics. One day, while driving around the island, "they came upon several airfields, but when they drew closer, they realized that all of the planes and equipment were fake, made of plywood, an elaborate ruse designed to fool Japanese reconnaissance planes" (70).

The *Super Man* crew finally gets their first real assignment. They set out with 25 other planes to bomb Wake Atoll, where the Japanese have built an army base.

Focus Question

Hillenbrand uses similes and metaphors to describe the B-24. Choose one and explain the comparison she makes. What makes this comparison effective? Why does Hillenbrand give the reader these details? How do they help the reader understand the story better?

Vocabulary

Word	Definition	Context clues: How did you figure out this word?
onslaught (51)		
recessive (55)		
abrasive (57)		
bonhomie (57)		
cheek by jowl (59)		

"War in the Pacific"

Quotes

In 1937, military leaders controlled Japan. In July, the Japanese launched an all-out war to take over China. The Japanese conquered much of eastern China, but by 1939, the two countries had fought to a stalemate. ("War in the Pacific")

The United States sided with China against Japan. ("War in the Pacific")

By August 1940, Japanese troops occupied the northern part of French Indochina (now Vietnam). ("War in the Pacific")

In July 1941, the Japanese occupied the southern part of Indochina. ("War in the Pacific")

The Japanese had a large, modern navy and an army hardened by years of combat in China. They hoped that many quick victories over the Americans and British would force peace, leaving Japan in control of eastern Asia and the western Pacific. ("War in the Pacific")

Roosevelt, busy aiding Britain in its war against Germany, ordered a freeze on trade with Japan. ("War in the Pacific")

Japan had little oil of its own; without oil and gasoline from the United States, its army and navy could not fight. ("War in the Pacific")

If Japan withdrew from China, American trade would resume, but the proud Japanese army would be humiliated. If the Japanese remained in China, Japan would need a new source of oil. ("War in the Pacific")

As the Japanese prepared for war, the Tojo government continued negotiating with the United States, hoping that Roosevelt might change his mind and resume trade with Japan. ("War in the Pacific")

In May 1940, [Roosevelt] stationed the U.S. Pacific Fleet at Pearl Harbor, Hawaii, as a further warning to Japan. ("War in the Pacific")

In September [1940], Japan signed a treaty of cooperation with Germany and Italy, whose armies were busy overrunning Europe and North Africa. Roosevelt [was] busy aiding Britain in its war against Germany. ("War in the Pacific")

The United States demanded that Japan withdraw from both Indochina and China. Roosevelt was confident that the Japanese would not risk attacking the powerful United States. ("War in the Pacific")

As negotiations continued in the fall of 1941, the U.S. Army and Navy rushed to reinforce Hawaii and the Philippine Islands. ("War in the Pacific")

Analyzing Perspectives Recording Form

Name: _____

Date: _____

Text	Japan's Role in Asia and the Pacific	U.S. Embargo of Japan	Diplomacy and the Failure of Diplomacy
"War in the Pacific"	What relationship did Japan want with the countries in Asia and the Pacific?	What was the U.S. embargo of Japan?	What was the relationship between the United States and Japan like leading up to Pearl Harbor?
"Day of Infamy" speech	What was Roosevelt's perspective on Japanese imperialism?	Why might Roosevelt not have mentioned the U.S. embargo of Japan in his speech?	What was Roosevelt's perspective on the relationship between the United States and Japan leading up to Pearl Harbor?
"Fourteen-Part Message"	What was the Japanese government's perspective on Japanese imperialism?	What was the Japanese government's perspective on the U.S. embargo?	What was the Japanese government's perspective on the relationship between the United States and Japan leading up to Pearl Harbor?

"Day of Infamy"

Quotes

Yesterday, the Japanese government also launched an attack against Malaya. Last night, Japanese forces attacked Hong Kong. Last night, Japanese forces attacked Guam. ("Day of Infamy" speech)

Last night, Japanese forces attacked the Philippine Islands. Last night, the Japanese attacked Wake Island. And this morning, the Japanese attacked Midway Island. ("Day of Infamy" speech)

Japan has, therefore, undertaken a surprise offensive extending throughout the Pacific area. ("Day of Infamy" speech)

The United States of America was suddenly and deliberately attacked by naval and air forces of the Empire of Japan. ("Day of Infamy" speech)

Indeed, one hour after Japanese air squadrons had commenced bombing in the American island of Oahu, the Japanese ambassador to the United States and his colleague delivered to our Secretary of State a formal reply to a recent American message. And while this reply stated that it seemed useless to continue the existing diplomatic negotiations, it contained no threat or hint of war or of armed attack. ("Day of Infamy" speech)

During the intervening time, the Japanese government has deliberately sought to deceive the United States by false statements and expressions of hope for continued peace. ("Day of Infamy" speech)

The United States was at peace with that nation and, at the solicitation of Japan, was still in conversation with its government and its emperor looking toward the maintenance of peace in the Pacific. ("Day of Infamy" speech)

I ask that the Congress declare that since the unprovoked and dastardly attack by Japan on Sunday, December 7th, 1941, a state of war has existed between the United States and the Japanese empire. ("Day of Infamy" speech)

"Fourteen-Part Message"

Quotes

The Japanese Government wants to insure the stability of East Asia and to promote world peace and thereby to enable each nation to find its proper place in the world. ("Fourteen-Part Message")

Ever since Japan's war with China, the Japanese Government has tried to restore peace. ("Fourteen-Part Message")

Obviously, the American Government's intention is to obstruct Japan's effort toward the establishment of peace through the creation of a new order in East Asia, and especially to preserve American interests by keeping Japan and China at war. ("Fourteen-Part Message")

The American Government objects to settling international issues through military pressure, but it uses economic pressure instead. ("Fourteen-Part Message")

Using economic pressure to deal with international relations should be condemned. It is, at times, more inhumane than military pressure. ("Fourteen-Part Message")

The government of Japan genuinely wants to come to a friendly understanding with the Government of the United States so that the two countries may secure peace in the Pacific Area and contribute toward world peace. Japan has continued sincere negotiations with the Government of the United States since last April. ("Fourteen-Part Message")

Last August, the Premier of Japan proposed to meet the President of the United States for a discussion of important problems between the two countries. However, the American Government insisted that the meeting should take place after an agreement of view had been reached on fundamental and essential questions. ("Fourteen-Part Message")

It is impossible not to reach the conclusion that the American Government desires to maintain and strengthen its dominant position in East Asia. The Japanese Government cannot tolerate that, since it directly runs counter to Japan's fundamental policy to enable each nation to enjoy its proper place in the world. ("Fourteen-Part Message")

Thus, the earnest hope of the Japanese Government to preserve the peace of the Pacific through cooperation with the American Government has finally been lost. The Japanese Government regrets to have to notify the American Government that it seems it is impossible to reach an agreement through further negotiations. ("Fourteen-Part Message")

EXPEDITIONARY
LEARNING

Mid-Unit Assessment: Fishbowl Note-Catcher

Understanding Perspectives on the Pearl Harbor Attack, "Day of Infamy" Version

Name: _____

Date: _____

Part A: Speaking Notes

Directions: Reread Roosevelt's "Day of Infamy" speech and answer the following questions to prepare for the Fishbowl discussion.

What did FDR accuse Japan of doing?	
What was FDR's perspective on the Pearl Harbor attack? What in the text makes you think as you do?	
What are some of the ways the speech you studied might affect people? What makes you think so? Make sure to use the strongest evidence from the speech and your common sense to respond to the question. Think about how hearing the speech might have affected: • People in the American military • People of Japanese descent living in the United States • People who lived in Hawaii	

Part B: Fishbowl Listening Notes

Directions: As you listen to the information being shared in the inside circle, answer the following questions.

What information is new to you?	
What thinking is new to you?	
What questions do you have?	

Part C: Follow-up Partner Discussion Notes

Directions: These two perspectives had an impact on individuals and societies. After studying both perspectives on the Pearl Harbor attack, analyze both perspectives by answering the question below and discussing your answer with your partner.

What are the overall differences in perspective? Use the best evidence to support your answer.

Part D: Post-Fishbowl Homework

Exit Ticket: Varying Perspectives

Select one of the following scenarios and write a response. Use evidence from the texts and common sense to support your answer.

- If you were an American citizen listening to FDR's speech, how might it affect you?
- If you were a Japanese citizen listening to FDR's speech, how might it affect you?
- If you were a Japanese citizen reading the Japanese message, how might it affect you?
- If you were an American citizen reading the Japanese message, how might it affect you?

_____

_____

_____

_____

_____

_____

_____

_____

Mid-Unit Assessment: Fishbowl Note-Catcher

Understanding Perspectives on the Pearl Harbor Attack, "Fourteen-Part Message" Version

Name: _____

Date: _____

Part A: Speaking Notes

Directions: Reread the "Fourteen-Part Message" and answer the following questions to prepare for the Fishbowl discussion.

What did the Japanese government accuse the United States of doing?	
What was the Japanese government's perspective on the Pearl Harbor attack? What in the text makes you think as you do?	
What are some of the ways the message you studied might affect people? What makes you think so? Make sure to use the strongest evidence from the text and your common sense to respond to the question. Think about how reading the text might have affected: • People in the Japanese military • People in Japan who had family living in the United States • People in Japan or the United States who had sons of draft age	

Part B: Fishbowl Listening Notes

Directions: As you listen to the information being shared in the inside circle, answer the following questions.

What information is new to you?	
What thinking is new to you?	
What questions do you have?	

Part C: Follow-up Partner Discussion Notes

Directions: These two perspectives had an impact on individuals and societies. After studying both perspectives on the Pearl Harbor attack, analyze both perspectives by answering the question below and discussing your answer with your partner.

What are the overall differences in perspective? Use the best evidence to support your answer.

Part D: Post-Fishbowl Homework

Exit Ticket: Varying Perspectives

Select one of the following scenarios and write a response. Use evidence from the texts and common sense to support your answer.

- If you were an American citizen listening to FDR's speech, how might it affect you?
- If you were a Japanese citizen listening to FDR's speech, how might it affect you?
- If you were a Japanese citizen reading the Japanese message, how might it affect you?
- If you were an American citizen reading the Japanese message, how might it affect you?

_____

_____

_____

_____

_____

_____

_____

Active and Passive Sentences

Name: _____

Date: _____

Active Voice: In most sentences with an action verb, the subject "does" or "acts on" the verb. Examples:

- John washed dishes.
- Kittens chased Rosa.

Passive Voice: Sentences can be changed so that the subject is being "acted on." Examples:

- The dishes were washed by John.
- Rosa was chased.

Tip: Insert the prepositional phrase "by _____" after the verb as a quick check for passive or active voice. If it makes no sense, the sentence is probably active. If it does make sense, it's probably passive.

He ate (by _____) hamburgers.

Doesn't make sense=ACTIVE

Hamburgers were eaten (by _____).

Makes sense (in a funny way)=PASSIVE

On the line, identify whether the sentences from *Unbroken* are in active or passive voice.

_____ "As he lost his aloof, thorny manner, he was welcomed by the fashionable crowd" (17).

_____ "The British were driven from Malaya and into surrender in Singapore in seventy days" (52).

_____ "For three days, the Japanese bombed and strafed the atoll" (52).

_____ "Louie was trained in the use of two bombsights" (53).

_____ "Then they were discovered by the railroad detective, who forced them to jump from the moving train at gunpoint" (15).

_____ "Phillips had one consuming passion" (57).

Unbroken Structured Notes

Pages 73–113

Name: _____

Date: _____

What is the gist of pages 73–77?

Summary of Pages 78–85

In early 1943, Louie is shaken by the deaths of several dozen men he knew. Some had crashed their planes, others had survived crashes but been eaten by sharks, and others had simply disappeared while on missions. One plane exploded when fuel leaked all over the floor and caught fire midflight.

These losses were not unusual:

In the Air Corps, 35,946 personnel died in nonbattle situations, the vast majority of them in accidental crashes. Even in combat, airmen appeared to have been more likely to die from accidents than combat itself. A report issued by the AAF surgeon general suggests that in the Fifteenth Air Force, between November 1, 1943, and May 25, 1945, 70 percent of men listed as killed in action died in operational aircraft accidents, not as a result of enemy action (80).

Aside from accidents, American airmen also face danger from Japanese fighters. The Japanese fly planes called Zeros, which are fast and attack with machine guns and cannon shells.

In addition to the airmen who were killed in accidents or by Japanese fighters, thousands disappeared and were never found. They may have died in the ocean, been captured by the enemy, or survived and been lost in unknown lands. "Unable to find them, the military declared them missing. If they weren't found within thirteen months, they were declared dead" (85).

What is the gist of pages 85–89?

Summary of Pages 90–113

(Note: Refer to the picture on page 111 of Super Man *with the damage done by the Japanese Zeros.)*

Louie and the crew of *Super Man* are sent to Canton Air Base and prepare to fly two missions over the Gilbert Islands. During the first mission, the fuel gauges "had settled unusually low," and the plane barely makes it back to Canton. Later on, the crew flies a rescue mission looking for a B-25 and its crew members that have gone down. They find the men in a life raft encircled by hundreds of sharks. Louie and Phil realize just how lethal "ditching" a plane into the ocean would be.

Their next mission is the bombing of Nauru, where they successfully hit all of their targets, but the plane is gravely wounded. Phil is forced to land *Super Man* on Funafuti Island with no hydraulic brakes, which he manages to do successfully. When the plane and its crew are assessed for damages, they find 594 bullet holes and several wounded crew members. Both Brooks and *Super Man* die that day.

While the crew is recuperating on Funafuti, the island comes under Japanese attack from "The Stinking Six." A pilot later recalled that "it sounded like the whole island was blowing up" (108). Phil and Louie take cover under a native hut and survive the bombings. Three B-24s are destroyed, and several casualties result from the attack.

Because *Super Man* and several members of its crew are out of commission, Louie, Phil, and the remaining healthy crew are transferred to the 42nd Squadron of the 11th Bomb Group, stationed in Oahu. Louie writes in his diary, "Every time they mix a crew, they have a crack up" (112). Shortly after they arrive in Oahu, Louie and Phil see their next plane, the *Green Hornet*. Neither man wants to fly in this plane.

Focus Question

On pages 85–89, why do you think Hillenbrand describes what the airmen fear in such detail? What does it help the reader understand about Louie and the men with whom he served? Use the strongest evidence from the book to support your answer.

Vocabulary

Word	Definition	Context clues: How did you figure out this word?
engulfed (74)		
garish (74)		
feted (76)		
lauded (77)		
delusory (88)		

Vocabulary Strips

Name: _____

Date: _____

onslaught (51)

----

recessive (55)

----

abrasive (57)

----

bonhomie (57)

----

engulfed (74)

----

garish (74)

----

feted (76)

----

lauded (77)

----

delusory (88)

Written Conversation Note-Catcher

Name: _____

Date: _____

Think about pages 85–89 and review the focus question from your *Unbroken* structured notes, pages 73–133: "On pages 85–89, why do you think Hillenbrand describes what the airmen fear in such detail? What does it help the reader understand about Louie and the men with whom he served? Use the strongest evidence from the book to support your answer." What was the most dangerous for downed airmen? Why?

I Say	My Partner Responds	I Build	My Partner Concludes

Active and Passive Sentences II

Name: _____

Date: _____

Example from *Unbroken*	How does the active or passive voice aid or construct meaning?
1. "Then they were discovered by the railroad detective, who forced them to jump from the moving train at gunpoint" (15). (Passive)	
2. "As he lost his aloof, thorny manner, he was welcomed by the fashionable crowd" (17). (Passive)	
3. "The British were driven from Malaya and into surrender in Singapore in seventy days" (52). (Passive)	
4. "For three days, the Japanese bombed and strafed the atoll" (52). (Active)	
5. "Louie was trained in the use of two bombsights" (53). (Passive)	
6. "Phillips had one consuming passion" (57). (Active)	

Things Good Writers Do Note-Catcher

Name: _____

Date: _____

Example from *Unbroken*	Technique	How does this technique contribute to tone or meaning?
"Then they were discovered by the railroad detective, who forced them to jump from the moving train at gunpoint" (15).		
"For three days, the Japanese bombed and strafed the atoll" (52).		

Fishbowl Discussion Rubric and Goal-Setting Sheet

The Pearl Harbor Attack

Criteria	Score				
	4	**3**	**2**	**1**	**0**
PREPARATION AND EVIDENCE (SL.8.1a)	Student brings thorough, relevant, well-organized notes, including evidence from informational texts, to the discussion.	Student brings relevant notes, including evidence from informational texts, to the discussion.	Student brings notes, including evidence from informational texts, to the discussion.	Student brings notes, including evidence from one informational text, to the discussion.	Student does not bring notes to the discussion.
	Student explicitly and consistently draws on relevant, compelling textual evidence during the discussion. Student uses evidence to probe and reflect on the ideas under discussion.	Student explicitly and consistently draws on relevant textual evidence during the discussion. Student uses evidence to probe and reflect on the ideas under discussion.	Student explicitly draws on some relevant textual evidence during the discussion. Student uses evidence to probe OR reflect on the ideas under discussion.	Student draws on little relevant textual evidence during the discussion.	Student does not draw on textual evidence during the discussion.

Criteria					
EFFECTIVE COMMUNICATION (SL.8.1b, c, e)	Student actively helps lead the discussion by: • Engaging in relevant conversation • Asking relevant questions • Listening actively • Responding to the ideas of others • Making eye contact • Maintaining a respectful tone and volume • Drawing peers into the discussion	Student actively participates in the discussion by: • Engaging in relevant conversation • Asking relevant questions • Listening actively • Making eye contact • Maintaining a respectful tone and volume	Student participates in the discussion but: • Is sometimes off-topic • Asks some irrelevant questions • Has some side conversations • Does not always make eye contact • Does not always maintain a respectful tone and volume	Student participates in the discussion but: • Is often off-topic • Asks irrelevant questions • Has frequent side conversations • Does not usually make eye contact • Does not usually maintain a respectful tone and volume	Student does not participate in the discussion.
RESPECTING MULTIPLE PERSPECTIVES (SL.8.1c, d, e)	Student considers others' diverse perspectives during the discussion by paraphrasing and asking respectful questions. Student always maintains respect while advocating for his or her opinion.	Student considers others' diverse perspectives during the discussion by paraphrasing or asking respectful questions. Student usually maintains respect while advocating for his or her opinion.	Student attempts to consider others' diverse perspectives during the discussion but has difficulty paraphrasing or asking respectful questions. Student sometimes maintains respect while advocating for his or her opinion.	Student does not consider others' perspectives during the discussion. Student has difficulty maintaining respect while advocating for his or her opinion.	Student does not participate in the discussion.

A student who does not participate in the discussion should be given a 0.

A student whose contributions to the discussion are only personal and make no reference to textual evidence can be scored no higher than a 1.

Using this rubric, set two or three goals for yourself. What would you like to work on improving during this Fishbowl discussion? (Examples: "I want to use my notes during the discussion," "I want to make eye contact with other people during the discussion.")

Goal No. 1:	Goal No. 2:	Goal No. 3:
What I did well:	What I did well:	What I did well:
How I can improve next time:	How I can improve next time:	How I can improve next time:

Fishbowl Sentence Starters

To paraphrase someone else's idea to make sure you understand, use:

I hear that you said . . .

To ask a question or probe, use:

I'm wondering . . .

I hear that you said . . . , and I'm still wondering . . .

Can you clarify what you meant when you said . . . ?

What you said about . . . raised a question for me. My question is . . . ?

It seems like what you said about . . . is different from what [someone else] said. (Name conflicting ideas)

To show how something has changed your thinking, use:

Now that I know that, I need to change what I think about . . .

To cite text evidence, use:

I hear that you said . . . , but I still think . . . because the text says . . . (Cite evidence)

What you said about . . . reminded me of something I read in the text. (Cite evidence)

End-of-Unit Assessment: Fishbowl Discussion, Part 1

Comparing Conflicting Accounts of the Pearl Harbor Attack

Name: _____

Date: _____

Questions for Discussion

- From your perspective, what was the gist of this text?

- What did FDR accuse Japan of doing?

- What was FDR's perspective on the Pearl Harbor attack?

- What key facts did FDR use in his speech? How did he interpret each of these facts?

- Are there any key facts that FDR omitted?

- What questions do you have for other people in the circle about their understanding of this text?

Unbroken Structured Notes

Pages 114–140

Name: _____

Date: _____

What is the gist of pages 114–121 and 125–130?

Summary of Pages 131–140

The military begins searching for the *Green Hornet* and its crew, knowing that the search area is enormous and the odds of finding the crew very long. Louie, Phil, and Mac see a B-25 and a B-24 from their rafts, but the planes do not see them. The men realize that they are drifting west, out of friendly territory, and hopes of being rescued are getting slim.

Mac eats all the chocolate when Louie and Phil are asleep, but Louie does not reprimand him. Their bodies are in distress, and with the fresh water gone, Mac begins to decline. Louie prays for the first time since his childhood.

At home, telegrams are sent to families of the *Green Hornet* crew.

"I regret to inform you that the commanding general Pacific area reports your son—First Lieutenant Russell A. Phillips—missing since May Twenty-seven. If further details or other information of his status are received you will be promptly notified" (138).

The entire Zamperini family remains resolute that Louie is alive.

Focus Question

From pages 119–121, the scene Hillenbrand describes is mostly underwater. What descriptive details does she use to vividly create this scene? How does this contribute to the meaning of the story? How is war affecting Louie in this mostly underwater scene?

Vocabulary

Word	Definition	Context clues: How did you figure out this word?
musher (115)		
assented (117)		
writhing (120)		
grossly (127)		
addled resolution (130)		

End-of-Unit Assessment: Fishbowl Discussion, Part 2

Comparing Conflicting Accounts of the Pearl Harbor Attack

Name: _____

Date: _____

- From your perspective, what was the gist of this text?

- What did the Japanese government accuse the United States of doing?

- What was the Japanese government's perspective on the Pearl Harbor attack?

- What key facts did the Japanese government use in this text? How were each of these facts interpreted?

- Are there any key facts that the Japanese government omitted?

- What questions do you have for other people in the circle about their understanding of this text?

EXPEDITIONARY
LEARNING

Exit Ticket: Fishbowl Discussion Wrap-Up

Name: _____

Date: _____

Part A.

Select one of the following scenarios and write a one-paragraph response. Use evidence from the texts and common sense to support your answer.

- If you were an American citizen listening to FDR's speech, how would it affect you?
- If you were a Japanese citizen listening to FDR's speech, how would it affect you?
- If you were a Japanese citizen reading the Japanese message, how would it affect you?
- If you were an American citizen reading the Japanese message, how would it affect you?

Part B.

Respond to the following question in a one-paragraph response. Use evidence from the texts and common sense to support your answer:

- After having read about the crash of the *Green Hornet* and the situation Louie finds himself in, why is it important to understand these two perspectives on the war?

Unbroken Structured Notes

Pages 141–168

Name: _____

Date: _____

Summary of Pages 141–147

The sharks continue to be a concern, but the lack of drinkable water is an even greater threat. During the first short rainfall, the men rig an ingenious way to collect and save the water. An albatross lands on Louie's head, and he is able to catch it. The men try to eat the bird, but the smell is overwhelming. Instead, they use the bird meat as bait and catch their first fish.

Louie reflects that the record for survival at sea is 34 days and hopes they will not have to break the record. He becomes concerned with the sanity of the men and turns the raft into a quiz show.

Louie and Phil remain optimistic, but Mac is not. They ward off their fears and focus on survival. Louie appears to have been wired for optimism, and Phil's deeply held religious beliefs keep him going. Mac has never been faced with a crisis or adversity in his life, and he is struggling to survive.

What is the gist of what you read on pages 141–147?

Summary of Pages 147–156

Louie, Phil, and Mac reach day 21 on the raft as they struggle to stay alive with limited food, water, and shelter from the sun. The men realize they will not be able to stay alive much longer, and Louie prays that if God will quench their thirst he will serve him forever. The next day it rains.

The men wish for a plane to come, and on the 27th day a plane comes. They realize it is not the rescue plane they are hoping for when it opens fire on them. Bullets pelt the raft, and Louie jumps overboard, risking his luck with the sharks to save himself from the bullets. While underwater, he looks down and can see the huge, gaping mouth of a shark racing toward him from the depths of the ocean. Louie dodges the shark, and as soon as the bullets stop, he pulls himself back into the raft. Phil and Mac lie curled up but alive and unhurt.

What is the gist of what you read on pages 147–156?

Summary of Pages 156–166

After the Japanese strafe the rafts, the sharks attack the rafts and the men. Louie is able to repair one raft, but the other is lost. Because of the direction the planes are flying, Louie and Phil are able to orient themselves and calculate that they will reach land after 46 or 47 days at sea. This means they need to survive three more weeks on the raft.

The sharks become aggressive and launch an attack on the men. Louie decides that if the sharks attack him, then he will attack the sharks. He catches and kills two sharks and shares their livers with Phil and Mac. A great white shark attacks the raft, and the men struggle to stay afloat. Mac saves Louie from the jaws of death. Eventually the great white gives up.

On day 33, Mac dies and the men bury him at sea. Louie prays for himself and Phil. He vows that "if God would save them, he would serve heaven forever" (165). The next day, Louie and Phil surpass the record of days survived at sea. They enter the doldrums, where Louie thinks, "Such beauty was too perfect to have come about by mere chance" (166).

What is the gist of what you read on pages 156–166?

Summary of Pages 166–168

On day 40, Louie is startled by the sound of a choir singing. He asks Phil if he hears anything, but Phil doesn't. Louie looks up and knows what he was hearing and seeing is impossible: 21 human figures singing a beautiful song in the clouds. Louie knows he is completely lucid and that this moment belongs only to him.

They drift for several more days, and they begin to notice that the sky is different. There are more birds. One morning, the waves churn and the horizon presents an ominous sight: an island.

What is the gist of what you read on pages 166–168?

Focus Question

"During Louie's ordeal of being lost at sea, Hillenbrand writes of several occasions in which he experiences the presence of God. What are these experiences like, and how does he experience God in each of them?"

Vocabulary

Word	Definition	Context clues: How did you figure out this word?
grotesque (148)		
demoralized (151)		
fickle (152)		
inept (156)		
lucid (167)		

Things Good Writers Do Note-Catcher

Name: _____

Date: _____

Example from *Unbroken*	Technique	How does this technique contribute to tone or meaning?
"Then they were discovered by the railroad detective, who forced them to jump from the moving train at gunpoint" (15). (Lesson 10)	Passive voice sentence	The person or thing being acted upon becomes the subject, almost more important than the person or thing completing the action.
"For three days, the Japanese bombed and strafed the atoll" (52). (Lesson 10)	Active voice	Easier to comprehend; the subject is completing the action.
The crash of the *Green Hornet* happens very quickly, but the author slows the scene down by providing rich, vivid details. (117–121)	Pacing	This slows the reader down to experience the details of the scene.

Survival at Sea Sentence Strips

"Louie came up with the ground rules. Each man would eat one square of chocolate in the morning, one in the evening. Louie allotted one water tin per man, with each man allowed two or three sips a day" (128–129).

"Louie kept his hand on Phil's head, stanching the bleeding" (129).

"Louie decided to divvy up breakfast, a single square of chocolate. He untied the raft pocket and looked in. All of the chocolate was gone . . . His gaze paused on Mac . . . The realization that Mac had eaten all of the chocolate rolled hard over Louie . . . Louie knew they couldn't survive long without food, but he quelled the thought . . . Curbing his irritation, Louie told Mac that he was disappointed in him. Understanding that Mac had acted in a panic, he reassured him that they'd soon be rescued. Mac said nothing" (132).

"Louie lunged for the raft pocket, retrieved the flare gun, and loaded a flare cartridge . . . He squeezed the trigger, the gun bucked in his hand . . . Louie dug out a dye pack and shook it hurriedly into the water, and a pool of vivid greenish-yellow bloomed over the ocean" (133).

"For a moment, Louie felt furious with the airmen who had passed so close to them, yet had not seen them. But his anger soon cooled . . . He knew how hard it was to see a raft, especially among clouds" (134).

"The castaways' bodies were declining" (135).

"Sometime on the fifth day, Mac snapped . . . He suddenly began screaming that they were going to die. Wild-eyed and raving, he couldn't stop shouting. Louie slapped him across the face. Mac abruptly went silent and lay down" (136).

"That night, before he tried to sleep, Louie prayed . . . He pleaded for help" (136).

"They had to find a way to save the water . . . Louie tried a new technique . . . He began continuously sucking the captured water into his mouth, then spitting it in the cans. Once the cans were full, he kept harvesting the rain, giving one man a drink every thirty seconds or so" (142).

"The men were ravenous. It was not clear that Mac's binge on the chocolate . . . was a catastrophe. Louie resented Mac, and Mac seemed to know it. Though Mac never spoke of it, Louie sensed that he was consumed with guilt over what he had done" (142).

"Louie had demonstrated that if they were persistent and resourceful, they could catch food, and both he and Phil felt inspired. Only Mac remained unchanged" (143).

"Louie was determined that no matter what happened to their bodies, their minds would stay under their control. Within a few days of the crash, Louie began peppering the other two with questions on every conceivable subject" (145).

"From earliest childhood, Louie had regarded every limitation placed on him as a challenge to his wits, his resourcefulness, and his determination to rebel . . . Now, as he was cast into extremity, despair and death became the focus of his defiance. The same attributes that had made him the boy terror of Torrance were keeping him alive in the greatest struggle of his life" (148).

"Looking at the dead raft, Louie thought of a use for it. Using the pliers, he pulled apart the layers of canvas on the ruined raft, creating a large, light sheet. At last, they had a canopy to block the sun in daytime and the cold at night" (159).

"Louie was furious at the sharks. He had thought they had an understanding: The men would stay out of the sharks' turf—the water—and the sharks would stay off of theirs—the raft . . . He stewed all night, scowled hatefully at the sharks all day, and eventually made a decision. If the sharks were going to try to eat him, he was going to try to eat them" (161).

"For days, Louie lay over the side of the raft, fishhooks tied to his fingers, trying to catch another pilot fish. He caught none" (151).

"That evening, Phil heard a small voice. It was Mac, asking Louie if he was going to die. Louie looked over at Mac, who was watching him. Louie thought it would be disrespectful to lie to Mac, who might have something that he needed to say or do before life left him. Louie told him that he thought he'd die that night. Mac had no reaction. Phil and Louie lay down, put their arms around Mac, and went to sleep. Sometime that night, Louie was lifted from sleep by a breathy sound, a deep outrushing of air, slow and final" (164).

Unbroken Structured Notes

Pages 169–181

Name: _____

Date: _____

What is the gist of pages 169–175 and 179–181?

Focus Question

In what ways are Louie and Phil treated differently by each group of Japanese they meet in the early days of their imprisonment? Why might that be? Cite the strongest evidence from the text to support your thinking.

Vocabulary

Word	Definition	Context clues: How did you figure out this word?
embrace (170)		
chastised (172)		
gaped (173)		
heaved (174)		
yanked (174)		
stench (174)		

Word Connotation T-chart

Name: _____

Date: _____

Directions: Sort the following word pairs by writing them in either the positive or negative column.

embrace—grip

chastised—disciplined

gaped—stared

heaved—lifted

yanked—removed

stench—odor

Positive	Negative

Understanding Invisibility Note-Catcher

Name: _____

Date: _____

Definition	Examples
Literal—	
Figurative—	

Unbroken Structured Notes

Pages 181–188

Name: _____

Date: _____

What is the gist of pages 181–183 and 184–188?

Focus Question

Reread the last paragraph on page 182 through to the page break on page 183. According to Hillenbrand, dignity was the one thing that kept Louie and Phil going, and it was also the one thing the guards sought to destroy. What is dignity? According to the text, what makes dignity so powerful?

Vocabulary

Word	Definition	Context clues: How did you figure out this word?
degradation (182)		
dignity (182)		
dehumanized (182)		
wretchedness (182)		
debased (183)		

Dignity Word Web

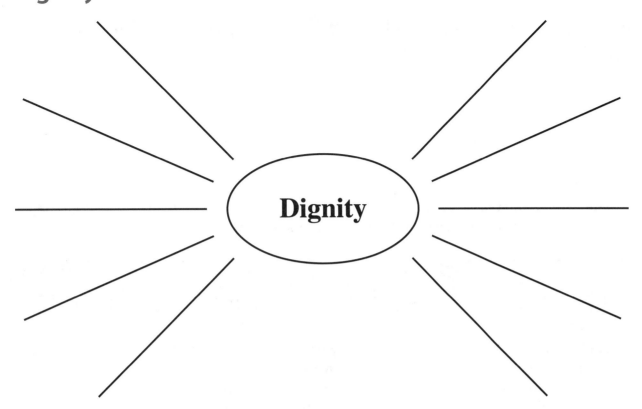

EXPEDITIONARY
LEARNING

Gathering Textual Evidence Note-Catcher

Informational Essay: The Invisibility of Captives during World War II

Name: _____

Date: _____

Louie Zamperini (Note-Catcher, Page 1)

Prompt: During World War II, what were the efforts to make both Japanese-American internees and American POWs in Japan "invisible," and how did each group resist?

Evidence	Page	Context	Explanation	Used in your writing?
Quotes from *Unbroken*, which show the strongest evidence of how the Japanese guards try to make Louie and the other POWs invisible.		A quick reminder of where and when this quote appears in the text. You may want to include an event, person, or group to which the quote connects.	Explain how this quote is evidence of being made invisible. Is this an example of **dehumanization** or **isolation**? Explain.	

Evidence	Page	Context	Explanation	Used in your writing?
Quotes from *Unbroken,* which show the strongest evidence of how the Japanese guards try to make Louie and the other POWs invisible.		A quick reminder of where and when this quote appears in the text. You may want to include an event, person, or group to which the quote connects.	Explain how this quote is evidence of being made invisible. Is this an example of **dehumanization** or **isolation**? Explain.	

Louie Zamperini (Section 1)

Evidence	Page	Context	Explanation	Used in your writing?
Quotes from *Unbroken*, which show the strongest evidence of how the Japanese guards try to make Louie and the other POWs invisible.		A quick reminder of where and when this quote appears in the text. You may want to include an event, person, or group to which the quote connects.	Explain how this quote is evidence of being made invisible. Is this an example of **dehumanization** or **isolation**? Explain.	

Miné Okubo (Section 2)

Evidence	Page	Context	Explanation ●	Used in your writing?
Quotes from "The Life of Miné Okubo," or primary source documents, which show the strongest evidence of how Miné and other internees resist being made invisible.		A quick reminder of where and when this quote appears in the text. You may want to include an event, person, or group to which the quote connects.	Explain how this quote is evidence of being made invisible. Is this an example of **dehumanization** or **isolation**? Explain.	

Unbroken Structured Notes

Pages 189–197

Name: _____

Date: _____

What is the gist of pages 189–190?

What is the gist of pages 190–193?

What is the gist of pages 193–197?

Focus Question

On page 196, Hillenbrand uses an example from Frederick Douglass's autobiography. How does this allusion to an American slave help the reader understand Louie's experiences? Cite the strongest evidence from the text to support your thinking.

Vocabulary

Word	Definition	Context clues: How did you figure out this word?
haggard (193)		
sadism (194)		
fomented (195)		
taboo (196)		
reticence (197)		

Written Conversation Note-Catcher

Name: _____

Date: _____

Prompt 1: In the last paragraph on page 194, going on to the top of page 195, Hillenbrand describes one reason some Japanese guards may have been so brutal to prisoners of war. What was this reason, and why do you think it contributed to such brutality by some?

Prompt 2: In the first full paragraph on page 195, Hillenbrand describes the second reason some Japanese guards may have been brutal to prisoners of war. What was this second reason, and how may have this reason contributed to such brutality by some?

I Say	My Partner Responds	I Build	My Partner Concludes

Exit Ticket

Name: _____

Date: _____

Based on what you have read in *Unbroken* about Japanese society during the time of World War II, how did the value of surrender being a terrible thing contribute to the invisibility of captives? What evidence do we have here that war is an extreme event that can sometimes bring out the worst in people?

_____

_____

_____

_____

_____

_____

_____

_____

_____

_____

_____

_____

_____

_____

_____

_____

**EXPEDITIONARY
LEARNING**

"The Life of Miné Okubo"

Source: Written by Expeditionary Learning for instructional purposes.

Miné Okubo was born in Riverside, California, on June 27, 1912, the fourth of seven children. Both of her parents were Japanese immigrants, also known as "Issei" (see box). Her father, who had studied Japanese history, named her after a Japanese creation goddess, Mine (pronounced "mee-neh"). Unfortunately, many people called her "Minnie" because they didn't know the sacred origin of her name.

> **Issei** *(EE-say)*: Japanese people who had immigrated to the United States but were not U.S. citizens
>
> **Nisei** *(NEE-say)*: First-generation Japanese Americans born in the United States (the children of Issei)
>
> **Sansei** *(SAN-say)*: Second-generation Japanese Americans born in the United States (the children of Nisei)

As a Nisei child, Miné identified as an American citizen. Her parents, born in Japan, asked her if she wanted to go to a special school to learn how to speak Japanese. She responded, "I don't need to learn Japanese! I'm an American!" (Curtin).

Living up to her name, Miné was a creative, curious child. Her mother, a calligrapher, helped her develop her skills by giving Miné an art assignment: paint a different cat every day. Later, a teacher at Miné's high school encouraged her to illustrate for the school newspaper and become art editor of the yearbook.

While studying art at Riverside Community College, Miné thought about applying to the University of California at Berkeley, but she worried that her family would not be able to afford it. She applied anyway, and was awarded a scholarship to attend.

In 1938, after earning bachelor's and master's degrees from Berkeley, Miné received a fellowship to travel to Europe to study art. She bought a used bicycle in France and rode to and from the Louvre, a famous art museum in Paris. (She picked up an important "souvenir" in France, too—the accent mark over the letter "e" in her name, which she added to her signature.) She brought her bike with her across Europe and spent many days happily pedaling around with lunch and art supplies inside the bike's basket.

Meanwhile, in Germany, a new leader named Adolf Hitler and his National Socialist (Nazi) Party had risen to power. In 1934, Hitler had crowned himself Führer ("supreme leader") and was spreading his message about the superiority of the "pure," white German race (which he called "Aryan"). He wanted to spread the Aryan race by conquering other countries—and by "eliminating," or killing, Jewish people. Hitler called this the "Final Solution" to the Jewish "problem," but it is now known as the Holocaust. Hitler began secretly building up Germany's military and signing pacts with other countries (including Japan and Italy) to prepare for war. In 1938, as Miné traveled around Europe studying art, Hitler was preparing for war by secretly building up Germany's army.

Miné's European odyssey was cut short when she received a telegram from Riverside in 1939. Her mother was sick, and she had to go home. Miné was lucky to find a spot on an American-bound ship; Hitler's army had recently invaded Austria and Czechoslovakia, and people were fleeing Europe in preparation for war. Miné boarded the last ship leaving France for America. On September 1, 1939, while Miné was at sea heading home, Hitler's army invaded Poland, Britain and France declared war on Germany, and World War II had officially begun.

Back in California, Miné was hired by the U.S. Army to create mosaic and fresco murals in San Francisco and Oakland. She worked with a famous Mexican artist named Diego Rivera.

In 1940, Miné's mother died. Miné remembered her in a painting, "Mother and Cat/Miyo and Cat," which she painted in 1941.

Source: A72.74. Miné Okubo, *Miyo and Cat*, 1941. Tempera on masonite, 29.75 x 24 in. Collection of the Oakland Museum of California. Gift of the Collectors Gallery.

As war raged in Europe, Miné moved into an apartment with her younger brother, Toku. The United States had not officially entered World War II, although tensions between the U.S., Germany, and Japan were rising. Miné and Toku had no idea how drastically their lives were about to change.

On December 7, 1941, Japanese troops bombed an American naval base at Pearl Harbor, in Hawaii. One day after the Pearl Harbor attack, President Franklin Delano Roosevelt (FDR) declared war on Japan, launching the United States into World War II.

Suddenly, although Miné and Toku were American citizens, they were considered the enemy because of their Japanese heritage. Suspicion and fear about Japanese-American spies reached a fever pitch, despite a report published in the fall of 1941 to the contrary. The *Report on Japanese on the West Coast of the United States,* also known as the "Munson Report," assured America that "There is no Japanese 'problem' on the Coast. There will be no armed uprising of Japanese . . . [The Nisei] are universally estimated from 90 to 98 percent loyal to the United States" (Niiya).

In spite of the Munson Report's claims, the U.S. government decided to take action against Japanese-Americans to "protect" America. Years later, Miné explained some of the "precautions" taken against Japanese-Americans: "Contraband such as cameras, binoculars, short-wave radios, and firearms had to be turned over to the local police . . . It was Jap this and Jap that. Restricted areas were prescribed and many arrests and detentions of enemy aliens took place" (Okubo, 10).

On February 19, 1942, FDR signed Executive Order 9066, which stated, "The successful prosecution of the war requires every possible protection against espionage and against sabotage." To this end, the order gave the government power to "relocate" Japanese-Americans (now considered "enemy aliens") to specially designated areas. This policy became known as internment. Within three months of this order, 110,000 people of Japanese heritage were moved into internment camps scattered throughout the Western states.

On April 23, 1942, Miné and Toku were notified that they had three days to pack their belongings and report to an "assembly center" for relocation. The preparation orders said: "Evacuees must carry with them on departure for the Assembly Center, the following property:

- Bedding and linens (no mattress) for each member of the family;

- Toilet articles for each member of the family;

- Extra clothing for each member of the family;

- Sufficient knives, forks, spoons, plates, bowls, and cups for each member of the family;

- Essential personal effects for each member of the family.

All items carried will be securely packaged, tied, and plainly marked . . . The size and number of packages is limited to that which can be carried by the individual or family group" (Thomas). Anything that internees couldn't carry with them when they reported to the assembly centers had to be left behind: precious family mementos, beloved pets, jobs, and friends. They left home unsure whether they would ever be allowed to return.

When Miné and Toku arrived at the assembly center (actually a church in downtown Berkeley) on April 26, they saw guards at every entrance and surrounding the building. "A woman seated near the entrance gave me a card with No. 7 printed on it and told me to go inside and wait," Miné wrote later. Then she was called into a room for a detailed interview. "As a result of the interview," she wrote, "my family name was reduced to No. 13660. I was given several tags bearing the family number, and was then dismissed" (Okubo, 19). For the rest of their time in the internment camps, Miné and Toku were referred to by this number, not by their names. Guarded by soldiers with weapons, Miné and Toku boarded a bus and were driven to Tanforan, another assembly center. When they arrived at Tanforan, they were told to strip and then given a medical examination: "A nurse looked into my mouth with a flashlight and checked my arms to see if I had been vaccinated for smallpox," Miné wrote (Okubo, 31).

At Tanforan, a former horseracing track, Miné, Toku, and the other internees were housed in horse stables. Miné described the first time she saw her new home: "The place was in semidarkness; light barely came through the dirty window on either side of the entrance. A swinging half-door divided the 20-by-9-ft. stall into two rooms . . . Both rooms showed signs of a hurried whitewashing. Spider webs, horse hair, and hay had been whitewashed with the walls. Huge spikes and nails stuck out all over the walls. A two-inch layer of dust covered the floor" (Okubo, 35).

Inadequate and dangerous conditions were common in the camps. Some internees reported being housed in cafeterias and bathrooms because the camps were overcrowded. The camps were designed to keep Japanese-Americans isolated from the rest of the country in remote areas. This often meant that they were located in the middle of the desert, exposing internees to searing heat during the day, freezing cold at night, and rattlesnakes at any hour. In addition, many of the camps had been built quickly, like Tanforan, and were not finished by the time the first internees arrived. Due to unfinished bathrooms, some internees had to use outhouses, which were unsanitary and afforded little to no privacy. Finally, the presence of armed guards in the camps led to tragedy in a few cases when internees were killed for not obeying orders.

Miné and Toku lived under strict rules at Tanforan. Anyone leaving or entering the camp was subject to a mandatory search, and internees could only see visitors in a special room at the top of the grandstand. Miné wrote, "We were close to freedom and yet far from it . . . Streams of cars passed by all day. Guard towers and barbed wire surrounded the entire center. Guards were on duty day and night" (Okubo, 81). Internees were not allowed to have cameras, but Miné wanted to document what was happening inside the camps. She put her artistic talent to use making sketches of daily life inside the fences.

After six months, Miné and Toku were transferred to Topaz, an internment camp in the Utah desert. As at Tanforan, Miné experienced isolation from the outside world, a near-complete lack of privacy, and the feeling of being reduced to a number. She continued chronicling the internee experience, as well as writing letters to friends back home. She also taught an art class to children in the camp and illustrated the front cover of *Trek,* a magazine created by the internees. She took a chance by entering a Berkeley art contest through the mail, and she won.

As a result, across the country, the editors of New York's *Fortune* magazine saw some of Miné's artwork. They decided to hire her as an illustrator for a special April 1944 issue of their magazine featuring information on Japanese culture. But she had to act fast; *Fortune* had asked her to arrive within three days. She had to submit to extensive background and loyalty checks to get permission to leave Topaz. After being cleared to leave, she set off for New York, wondering how she would be able to readjust to life as a free person again.

EXPEDITIONARY
LEARNING

"The Life of Miné Okubo" Works Cited

(Most useful sources for students to use to learn about the end of Okubo's story are in **bold**.)

Burton, Jeffrey F., Mary M. Farrell, Florence B. Lord, and Richard W. Lord. "Chapter 1: Sites of Shame: An Introduction." In *Confinement and Ethnicity: An Overview of World War II Japanese American Relocation Sites*. National Park Service, Sept. 1, 2000. Accessed on April 15, 2013, http://www.nps.gov/history/history/online_books/anthropology74/ce1.htm.

Curtin, Mary H. "Riverside's Miné Okubo." In Splinters-Splinters (blog). Ed. George N. Giacoppe. August 27, 2011. Accessed on April 12, 2013. http://splinters-splinters.blogspot.com/2011/08/riversides-mine-okubo.html.

Executive Order No. 9066, 3 C.F.R. (1942).

Hastad, Chelsie, Louann Huebsch, Danny Kantar, and Kathryn Siewert. "Miné Okubo." Voices from the Gaps (University of Minnesota, May 3, 2004). Accessed on April 12, 2013. http://voices.cla.umn.edu/artistpages/okuboMine.php.

Ina, Satsuki. "Internment History." *Children of the Camps*. PBS, 1999. Accessed on April 15, 2013. http://www.pbs.org/childofcamp/history/index.html.

McIntyre, Edison. "War in the Pacific." *Cobblestone* 15, no. 1 (1994).

Niiya, Brian. "Munson Report." *Densho Encyclopedia*. March 19, 2013. Accessed on April 15, 2013. http://encyclopedia.densho.org/Munson_Report/.

Okubo, Miné. *Citizen 13660* (Seattle: University of Washington Press, 1983).

_____. *Mother and Cat|Miyo and Cat*. 1941. OCMA Collections, Oakland Museum of California, 2013. Accessed on April 12, 2013. http://collections.museumca.org/?q=collection-item/a7274.

Thomas, Rick. "Civilian Exclusion Order #5." *Japanese Internment*. In Time and Place, July 2008. Accessed on April 12, 2013. http://www.intimeandplace.org/Japanese Internment/images/exclusionorder.html.

Woo, Elaine. "Miné Okubo: Her Art Told of Internment." Los Angeles Times, March 4, 2001. Accessed on April 12, 2013, http://articles.latimes.com/2001/mar/04/local/me-33276.

"World War II." *History.com*. A&E Television Networks, 1996–2013. Accessed on April 12, 2013. http://www.history.com/topics/world-war-ii.

"The Life of Miné Okubo" Structured Notes

Name: _____

Date: _____

What is the gist of this text?

Focus Question

How did war affect Okubo? Cite two specific examples from the text to support your answer.

Vocabulary

Word	Definition	Context clues: How did you figure out this word?

Character Traits Graphic Organizer

Understanding Miné

Name: _____

Date: _____

Based on the information in this text, what are Miné Okubo's character traits?

Trait	Details from "The Life of Miné Okubo"

Character Traits Quick Write

Understanding Miné

Name: _____

Date: _____

In "The Life of Miné Okubo," Okubo describes being interviewed at the assembly center when she reported for internment: "As a result of the interview . . . my family name was reduced to No. 13660. I was given several tags bearing the family number, and was then dismissed." What can you infer about Okubo based on the way she describes these events?

_____

_____

_____

_____

_____

_____

_____

_____

_____

_____

_____

_____

_____

_____

_____

_____

Primary Sources

Japanese-American Internment during World War II

Name: _____

Date: _____

Historical Context: After the Japanese attack on Pearl Harbor on December 7, 1941, U.S. President Franklin D. Roosevelt signed an order forcing Japanese-American citizens to relocate to "internment camps." This internment was designed to prevent Japanese Americans, considered "enemy aliens" at that time, from attacking the United States from within its own borders. Over 110,000 Japanese Americans, mostly from the West Coast, were forced to live in internment camps until January 1945, when the order was rescinded and they were allowed to return home.

Source 1

Note: The term "fifth column" refers to people who are spies within their own country.

> The enemy alien problem on the Pacific Coast, or much more accurately the Fifth Column problem, is very serious and it is very special. What makes it so serious and so special is that the Pacific Coast is in imminent danger of a combined attack from within and from without . . . It is a fact that since the outbreak of the Japanese war there has been no important **sabotage** on the Pacific Coast . . . [T]his is not, as some have liked to think, a sign that there is nothing to be feared. It is a sign that the blow is well organized and that it is held back until it can be struck with maximum effect.

Source: Walter Lippmann, "Today and Tomorrow: The Fifth Column on the Coast," *Washington Post,* February 12, 1942. *http://encyclopedia .densho.org/sources/en-denshopd-i67–00001–1/.*

sabotage: deliberate destruction; an attack

1a. What is Lippmann's point of view on Japanese Americans? Cite one piece of evidence to support your answer.

_____

_____

_____

_____

_____

_____

1b. Would Lippmann have supported the establishment of Japanese-American internment camps during World War II? Cite one piece of evidence to support your answer.

_____

_____

_____

_____

_____

_____

Source 2

Note: In 1941, Curtis B. Munson investigated the loyalty of Japanese Americans. The following are excerpts from the report he submitted to President Roosevelt.

There are still Japanese in the United States who will tie dynamite around their waist and make a human bomb out of themselves. We grant this, but today they are few. The Nisei, who are the children of Japanese immigrants, are universally estimated from 90 to 98 percent loyal to the United States . . . The Nisei are pathetically eager to show this loyalty. They are not Japanese in culture. They are foreigners to Japan. Though American citizens they are not accepted by Americans, largely because they look differently and can be easily recognized . . . They are not oriental or mysterious, they are very American and are of a proud, self-respecting race suffering from a little inferiority complex and a lack of contact with the white boys they went to school with. They are eager for this contact and to work alongside them . . . There is no Japanese "problem" on the Coast. There will be no armed uprising of Japanese.

Source: Curtis B. Munson, "Report and Suggestions Regarding Handling the Japanese Question on the Coast," Commission on Wartime Relocation and Internment of Civilians, December 20, 1941. http://encyclopedia.densho.org/Munson_Report/.

2a. What is Munson's point of view on Japanese Americans? Cite one piece of evidence to support your answer.

_____

_____

_____

_____

_____

EXPEDITIONARY
LEARNING

2b. Would Munson have supported the establishment of Japanese-American internment camps during World War II? Cite one piece of evidence to support your answer.

_____

_____

_____

_____

_____

_____

Source 3

Note: The following are excerpts from President Roosevelt's order authorizing Japanese-American internment, February 19, 1942.

[T]he successful prosecution of the war requires every possible protection against **espionage** and against sabotage . . . Now, therefore, I hereby authorize and direct the Secretary of War to prescribe military areas from which any or all persons may be excluded, and with respect to which, the right of any person to enter, remain in, or leave shall be subject to whatever restrictions the Secretary of War may impose.

Source: President Franklin D. Roosevelt, "Executive Order 9066: Authorizing the Secretary of War to Prescribe Military Areas," The White House, February 19, 1942. Public domain.

espionage: spying

3a. What is Roosevelt's point of view on Japanese Americans? Cite one piece of evidence to support your answer.

_____

_____

_____

_____

_____

_____

_____

3b. Based on this source, why did Roosevelt support the establishment of Japanese-American internment camps during World War II? Cite one piece of evidence to support your answer.

_____

_____

_____

_____

_____

_____

Source 4

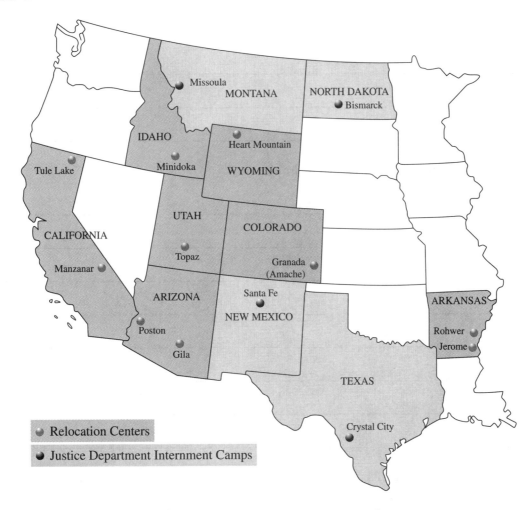

Map of Japanese-American Internment Camps

Source: National Park Service, "Map 2: War Relocation Centers in the United States." http://www.nps.gov/nr/twhp/wwwlps/lessons/89manzanar/89locate2.htm. Public domain.

4a. What do you notice about the location of the relocation centers and internment camps?

_____

_____

_____

_____

_____

_____

_____

_____

_____

_____

_____

4b. Why might the location of these camps be important?

_____

_____

_____

_____

_____

_____

_____

_____

_____

_____

_____

Source 5

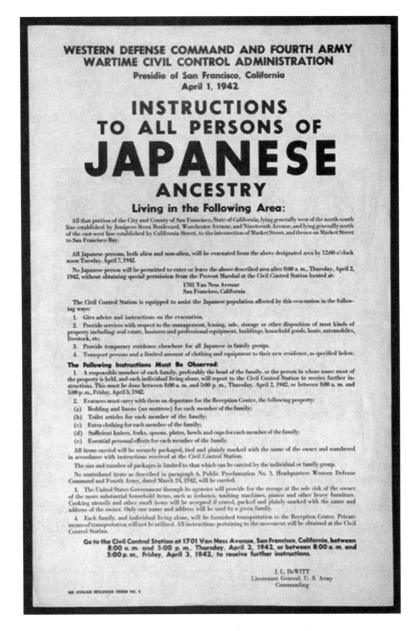

Source: "Exclusion Order posted at First and Front Streets in San Francisco directing removal of persons of Japanese ancestry from the first section of the city to be affected by evacuation. Evacuees will be housed in War Relocation Authority centers for the duration." Franklin Delano Roosevelt Presidential Library and Museum, Hyde Park, New York, April 1, 1942. Public domain.

5a. Based on this source, what is the author's point of view on Japanese Americans? Cite one piece of evidence to support your answer.

_____

_____

_____

Source 6

Note: Japanese-American internees were assigned identification numbers. These numbers were printed on tags and attached to each internee's clothing and belongings.

The Mochida Family Awaiting Relocation

Source: Series: Central Photographic File of the War Relocation Authority, compiled 1942–1945, Record Group 210: Records of the War Relocation Authority, 1941–1989, Department of the Interior, War Relocation Authority. Public domain. http://research.archives.gov/description/537505.

6a. Given what you know about Japanese-American internment from the previous sources, why do you think internees were required to wear identification tags during their relocation?

_____

_____

_____

_____

_____

_____

_____

_____

6b. Why do you think the photographer chose to include the family's last name (Mochida) in the picture and in the title?

_____

_____

_____

_____

_____

_____

6c. What do you think is the photographer's point of view on Japanese-American internment? Cite one piece of evidence to support your answer.

_____

_____

_____

_____

_____

_____

_____

Source 7

Note: This cartoon was published in response to Document 1. "TNT" is an explosive.

Source: Theodor Suess Giesel, Dr. Seuss Collection, University of California at San Diego Library, La Jolla, California.

7a. What is Dr. Seuss's point of view on Japanese Americans? Cite one piece of evidence to support your answer.

_____

_____

_____

_____

_____

_____

_____

_____

_____

7b. Would Dr. Seuss have supported the establishment of Japanese-American internment camps during World War II? Cite one piece of evidence to support your answer.

_____

_____

_____

_____

_____

_____

_____

_____

_____

_____

_____

Large Version of Primary Sources

Source 1

The enemy alien problem on the Pacific Coast, or much more accurately the Fifth Column problem, is very serious and it is very special. What makes it so serious and so special is that the Pacific Coast is in imminent danger of a combined attack from within and from without . . . It is a fact that since the outbreak of the Japanese war there has been no important sabotage on the Pacific Coast. From what we know about Hawaii and about the Fifth Column in Europe this is not, as some have liked to think, a sign that there is nothing to be feared. It is a sign that the blow is well organized and that it is held back until it can be struck with maximum effect.

Source: Walter Lippmann, "Today and Tomorrow: The Fifth Column on the Coast," *Washington Post,* February 12, 1942. *http://encyclopedia .densho.org/sources/en-denshopd-i67–00001–1/.*

Source 2

There are still Japanese in the United States who will tie dynamite around their waist and make a human bomb out of themselves. We grant this, but today they are few. The Nisei, who are the children of Japanese immigrants, are universally estimated from 90 to 98 percent loyal to the United States . . . The Nisei are pathetically eager to show this loyalty. They are not Japanese in culture. They are foreigners to Japan. Though American citizens they are not accepted by Americans, largely because they look differently and can be easily recognized . . . They are not oriental or mysterious, they are very American and are of a proud, self-respecting race suffering from a little inferiority complex and a lack of contact with the white boys they went to school with. They are eager for this contact and to work alongside them . . . There is no Japanese "problem" on the Coast. There will be no armed uprising of Japanese.

Source: Curtis B. Munson, "Report and Suggestions Regarding Handling the Japanese Question on the Coast," Commission on Wartime Relocation and Internment of Civilians, December 20, 1941. *http://encyclopedia.densho.org/Munson_Report/.*

Source 3

[T]he successful prosecution of the war requires every possible protection against espionage and against sabotage . . . Now, therefore, I hereby authorize and direct the Secretary of War to prescribe military areas from which any or all persons may be excluded, and with respect to which, the right of any person to enter, remain in, or leave shall be subject to whatever restrictions the Secretary of War may impose.

—Franklin D. Roosevelt

The White House,

February 19, 1942

Source: President Franklin D. Roosevelt, "Executive Order 9066: Authorizing the Secretary of War to Prescribe Military Areas," The White House, February 19, 1942. Public domain.

EXPEDITIONARY
LEARNING

Source 4

Map of Japanese-American Internment Camps

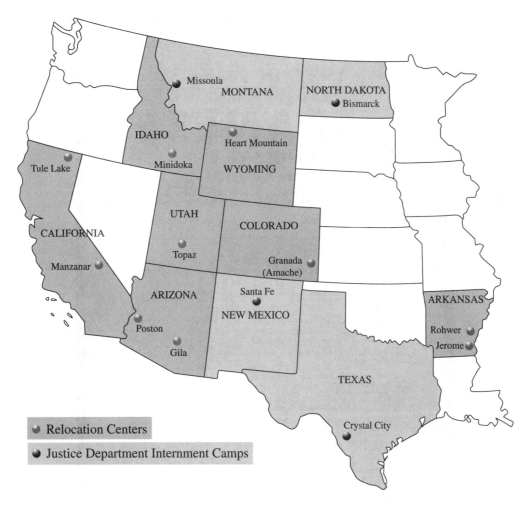

Source: National Park Service, "Map 2: War Relocation Centers in the United States." http://www.nps.gov/nr/twhp/wwwlps/lessons/89manzanar/89locate2.htm. Public domain.

Source 5

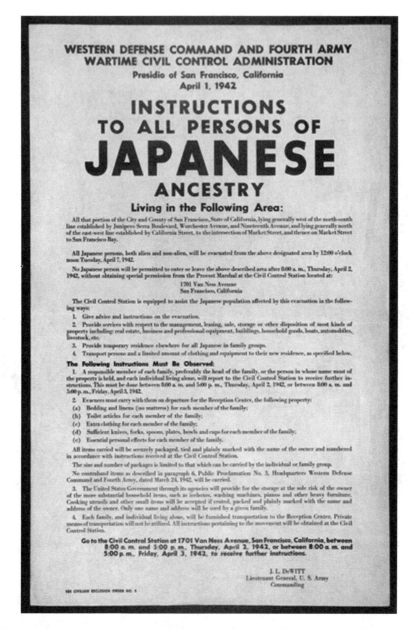

Source: "Exclusion Order posted at First and Front Streets in San Francisco directing removal of persons of Japanese ancestry from the first section of the city to be affected by evacuation. Evacuees will be housed in War Relocation Authority centers for the duration." Franklin Delano Roosevelt Presidential Library and Museum, Hyde Park, New York, April 1, 1942. Public domain.

Source 6

The Mochida Family Awaiting Relocation

Source: Series: Central Photographic File of the War Relocation Authority, compiled 1942–1945, Record Group 210: Records of the War Relocation Authority, 1941–1989, Department of the Interior, War Relocation Authority. Public domain. http://research.archives.gov/description/537505.

Source 7

Source: Theodor Suess Geisel, Dr. Seuss Collection, University of California at San Diego Library, La Jolla, California.

Source 8

Source: Miné Okubo, "Quotes," Citizen 13660 (Seattle: University of Washington Press, 1983).

Miné Okubo Quotes (from *Citizen 13660*)

"Contraband such as cameras, binoculars, short-wave radios, and firearms had to be turned over to the local police . . . It was Jap this and Jap that. Restricted areas were prescribed and many arrests and detentions of enemy aliens took place."

"A woman seated near the entrance gave me a card with No. 7 printed on it and told me to go inside and wait . . . As a result of the interview, my family name was reduced to No. 13660. I was given several tags bearing the family number, and was then dismissed."

"The place was in semidarkness; light barely came through the dirty window on either side of the entrance. A swinging half-door divided the 20-by-9 ft. stall into two rooms . . . Both rooms showed signs of a hurried whitewashing. Spider webs, horse hair, and hay had been whitewashed with the walls. Huge spikes and nails stuck out all over the walls. A two-inch layer of dust covered the floor."

"We were close to freedom and yet far from it . . . Streams of cars passed by all day. Guard towers and barbed wire surrounded the entire center. Guards were on duty day and night."

EXPEDITIONARY
LEARNING

Source Comparison Strips

Source __ disagrees with Source __ about _____ because:	
Source ___ says:	Source ___ says:

- -

Source __ disagrees with Source __ about _____ because:	
Source ___ says:	Source ___ says:

- -

Source __ disagrees with Source __ about _____ because:	
Source ___ says:	Source ___ says:

Primary Sources

Japanese-American Internment during World War II Quick Write

Name: _____

Date: _____

Quick Write: How can we understand Miné Okubo's story better based on the new information in these primary sources? Cite two specific details to support your answer.

_____

_____

_____

_____

_____

_____

_____

_____

_____

_____

_____

_____

_____

_____

_____

_____

_____

_____

EXPEDITIONARY
LEARNING

Analyzing Mediums

Name: _____

Date: _____

Medium: Text	
Advantages:	Disadvantages:

Medium: Photograph	
Advantages:	Disadvantages:

Medium: Cartoon	
Advantages:	Disadvantages:

Name: _____

Date: _____

Comparing Source 1 and Source 7

1. Source 1 and Source 7 share a point of view on Japanese Americans. What is that point of view?

_____

_____

_____

_____

2. What are the two different mediums the creators of these sources chose to use?

_____

_____

_____

_____

3. Why might Walter Lippmann, the author of Source 1, have chosen to use text as his medium? What are the advantages of using text to communicate his point of view about Japanese Americans?

_____

_____

_____

_____

4. Why might Dr. Seuss, the author of Source 7, have chosen to use a cartoon as his medium? What are the advantages of using a cartoon to communicate his point of view about Japanese Americans?

_____

_____

_____

_____

Name: _____

Date: _____

Comparing Source 4 and Source 8

5. Source 4 and the last two quotes of Source 8 are about the same topic. What is that topic?

_____

_____

_____

_____

6. What are the two different mediums the creators of these sources chose to use?

_____

_____

_____

_____

7. What can we learn about the internment camps from Source 4 that we cannot learn from Source 8?

_____

_____

_____

_____

8. What can we learn about the internment camps from Source 8 that we cannot learn from Source 4?

_____

_____

_____

_____

Venn Diagram

Miné and Louie

Name: _____

Date: _____

Louie Zamperini and Miné Okubo both experienced a form of captivity during World War II. Louie was a prisoner of war in Japan, and Miné was forced to move to an internment camp in the United States. Compare and contrast their experiences. Use specific details and evidence from *Unbroken* and "The Life of Miné Okubo" to fill in the Venn diagram:

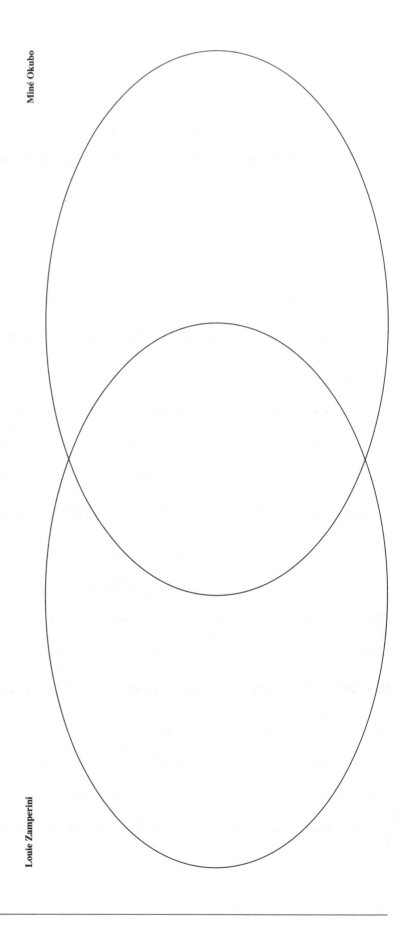

Louie Zamperini

Miné Okubo

Exit Ticket

Analyzing Mediums

Name: _____

Date: _____

The two sources that follow both communicate ideas about Japanese-American internment, but their creators have chosen to use different mediums to express these ideas. Beneath each source, explain at least one advantage and one disadvantage of using this medium to present these **specific** ideas.

Source: Series: Central Photographic File of the War Relocation Authority, compiled 1942–1945, Record Group 210: Records of the War Relocation Authority, 1941–1989, Department of the Interior, War Relocation Authority. Public domain. http://research.archives.gov /description/537505.

Medium:	
Advantages:	Disadvantages:

"A woman seated near the entrance gave me a card with No. 7 printed on it and told me to go inside and wait . . . As a result of the interview, my family name was reduced to No. 13660. I was given several tags bearing the family number, and was then dismissed."—Miné Okubo, *Citizen 13660*

Medium:	
Advantages:	Disadvantages:

Mid-Unit Assessment

Evaluating and Classifying Primary Sources

Name: _____

Date: _____

Learning Target: I can evaluate the advantages and disadvantages of using different mediums to present an idea. (RI.8.7)

Part A.

Directions: Take 10 minutes to silently browse and view the mediums used in the Gallery Walk. Then select three different mediums to analyze for this assessment.

1. Write the number of each medium you have selected.

2. Identify the type of each medium (remember, you must choose three different types).

3. Evaluate the advantages and disadvantages of using each type of medium.

Medium: No.:_____ Type:_____	
Advantages:	Disadvantages:

Medium: No.:_____ Type:_____	
Advantages:	Disadvantages:

Medium: No.:_____ Type:_____	
Advantages:	Disadvantages:

Part B.

Directions: Now that you have identified three different types of mediums and have evaluated the advantages and disadvantages of using each, respond to the question:

"From the perspective of the viewer, what can you learn from these different mediums? What is an advantage of using one medium over another to convey an idea?" Make sure to use the strongest examples from your previous work to support your answer.

_____

_____

_____

_____

_____

_____

_____

_____

_____

_____

_____

_____

_____

_____

_____

Unbroken Structured Notes

Pages 200–229

Name: _____

Date: _____

Summary of Pages 200–203

Louie meets Bill Harris in Ofuna and admires his intellect and courage as they all continue to struggle under inhumane treatment and malnutrition. Gaga the duck becomes the POWs' mascot. Jimmie Sasaki calls Louie into his office often, but no effort to interrogate him is ever made. Louie suspects that Sasaki is protecting him.

What is the gist of pages 203–210?

Summary of Pages 212–229

Both Louie's and Phil's families refuse to believe that their sons are dead. Even after an official letter from Hale's office tells them that Louie is dead and his trunk is shipped home, they hold on to their belief in Louie's survival. Thirteen months after their disappearance, messages were sent to the families of the *Green Hornet* crew. The letters officially declared all the men dead.

A Japanese document is found. When the document is translated, it shows that Louie and Phil were picked up, beaten, and then sent to Japan by boat. The families are not made aware of this.

Focus Question

The men imprisoned at Ofuna participate in small acts of rebellion and subversion. In what ways do they rebel, and what is the effect of these acts on the prisoners?

EXPEDITIONARY
LEARNING

Vocabulary

Word	Definition	Context clues: How did you figure out this word?
querying (203)		
clandestine (203)		
subversion (204)		
purloined (205)		
loitering (208)		

Short Response (2-Point) Holistic Rubric

Source: Based on a rubric created for the New York State Common Core Curriculum.

The features of a **2-point response** are:

- Valid inferences or claims from the text where required by the prompt

- Evidence of analysis of the text where required by the prompt

- Relevant facts, definitions, concrete details, or other information from the text to develop a response according to the requirements of the prompt

- Sufficient number of facts, definitions, concrete details, or other information from the text as required by the prompt

- Complete sentences in which errors do not affect readability

The features of a **1-point response** are:

- A mostly literal recounting of events or details from the text as required by the prompt

- Some relevant facts, definitions, concrete details, or other information from the text to develop a response according to the requirements of the prompt

- Incomplete sentences or bullets

The features of a **0-point response** are:

- A response that does not address any of the requirements of the prompt or is totally inaccurate

- No response (blank answer)

- A response that is not written in English

- A response that is unintelligible or indecipherable

Written Conversation Note-Catcher

Name: _____

Date: _____

The men imprisoned at Ofuna participate in small acts of rebellion and subversion. In what ways do they rebel? What is the effect of these acts on the prisoners?

I Say	My Partner Responds	I Build	My Partner Concludes

Conditional and Subjunctive Moods

Conditional Mood

Sentences written in the conditional mood indicate a state that will cause something to happen. Key words are *might, could,* and *would.* Examples:

- The soda might explode if you shake it up.
- The soda could explode if you keep shaking it.

Subjunctive Mood

Sentences written in the subjunctive mood indicate a state that is a wish, a desire, or an imaginary situation contrary to fact. Key words or phrases include *if, I wish, I hope that,* or *I desire that.* Examples:

- If he were to shake the soda, it would explode.
- I wish I were a butterfly.

TIP 1: The subjunctive mood requires use of "were" instead of "was" as in the examples above.

TIP 2: Sometimes sentences are conditional *and* subjunctive.

On the line, identify whether the sentences from *Unbroken* are in the conditional or subjunctive mood.

1. _____ "Residents looking out their back windows might catch a glimpse of a long-legged boy dashing down the alley, a whole cake balanced on his hands" (6).

2. _____ "If asked what he wanted to be, his answer would have been 'cowboy'" (11).

3. _____ "If Louie were recognized for doing something right, Pete argued, he'd turn his life around" (13).

4. _____ "It had been Mitchell's job to strap them to his body, but if he had done so, the instruments had gone to the bottom with him" (128).

5. _____ "Phil felt as if he were on fire" (141).

6. _____ "As a pilot, he was keenly conscious that if he made a mistake, eight other men could die" (90).

Unbroken Structured Notes

Pages 230–247

Name: _____

Date: _____

What's the gist of pages 230–234, 237–238, 239–242, and 244–247?

Summary of Pages 242–244

Louie and the enlisted men fight back in the only ways they can: sabotage and stealing. They risk their lives to sink barges, pee on rice, and derail trains, but they are no longer passive captives. They steal rice, sugar, and anything they can. "Stealing from the enemy won back their dignity" (244).

Focus Question

What does Hillenbrand see as the reasons the Bird is the way he is?

Vocabulary

Word	Definition	Context clues: How did you figure out this word?
imperious (232)		
nihilism (233)		
volatility (234)		
haughtiness (238)		
impunity (245)		

Word Choice Note-Catcher

Name: _____

Date: _____

Words and Phrases from *Unbroken*	How do these words help me understand Watanabe better?

Three Threes in a Row Note-Catcher

Name: _____

Date: _____

In what ways did Watanabe's actions reveal his belief in nihilism?	Why did Watanabe target Louie specifically?	What are some acts of dehumanization that Watanabe used to make Louie invisible?
What was the defining event that led to Watanabe's brutal behavior? How did it affect him?	What were the small acts of resistance the POWs waged at Omori?	How did Louie resist the Bird's attempts to dehumanize him to try to make him invisible (in both senses of the word)?
What two attributes separated Watanabe from the other prison guards?	Why were acts of sabotage and resistance important to the POWs?	In what ways was Louie isolated from the outside world and made invisible?

Unbroken Structured Notes

Pages 248–261

Name: _____

Date: _____

What is the gist of pages 248–253?

Summary of Pages 253–258

In 1944 an Office of War Information employee hears a Japanese propaganda show "Postman Calls" informing listeners that Louie is alive and in a Japanese POW camp. At the same time, the family is sent his Purple Heart and $10,000 in insurance money for his death. They choose to save the medal and the money for Louie's arrival home.

A second broadcast of "Postman Calls" is Louie himself speaking. He drops hints that would help his family identify him as the speaker. People from all over the country call the Zamperinis about the broadcast—many confirm it was Louie's voice.

What's the gist of "Louie's letter" on pages 256–257?

What is the gist of pages 259–261?

Focus Question

In what ways does Louie continue to resist invisibility?

Vocabulary

Word	Definition	Context clues: How did you figure out this word?
clamor (250)		
distorting (250)		
portended (251)		
vitriol (251)		
propaganda (260)		

Frayer Model

Propaganda

Name: _____

Date: _____

Understanding Propaganda

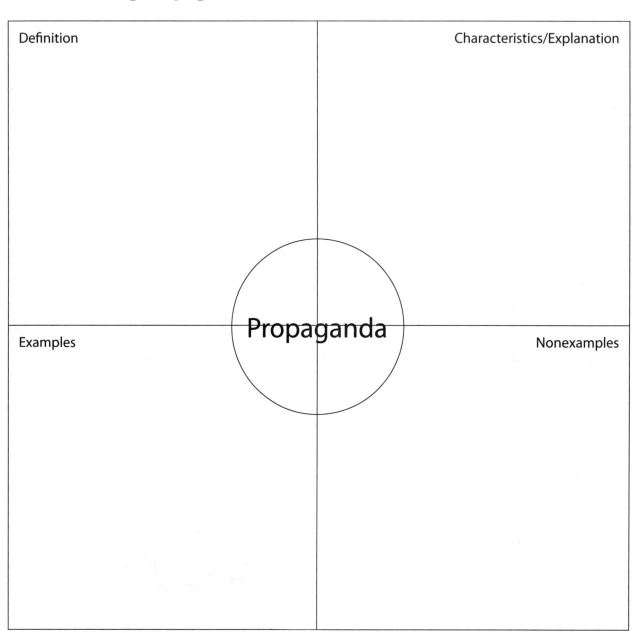

Definition	Characteristics/Explanation
Examples	Nonexamples

Propaganda

EXPEDITIONARY
LEARNING

Written Conversation Note-Catcher

Name: _____

Date: _____

During World War II, what did Louie Zamperini and Miné Okubo have in common?

I Say	My Partner Responds	I Build	My Partner Concludes

Unbroken Structured Notes

Pages 261–329

Name: _____

Date: _____

Summary of Pages 261–290

Still in the Omori POW camp, Louie and the other prisoners see U.S. B-29s flying overhead on their way to Tokyo. The bombers increase the Bird's mania, and he stalks Louie. Louie, starving, starts to unravel under the Bird's incessant attacks. Eventually, the Bird is ordered to leave Omori because of his cruelty toward the POWs. Bill Harris is transferred to Omori, where he and Louie are reunited. Bill is in rough shape, so Louie gives him his Red Cross box to help him regain his strength. The Tokyo bombings continue. The POWs hear about the "kill all" order and fear for their lives. Louie is transferred to Naoetsu, where the Bird is in command. The Bird withholds Red Cross packages and forces the POWs into slave labor. Louie fights back by stealing rice. He hurts himself working and is forced to work in the camp all day with the Bird, who makes him clean out a pig pen with his bare hands. Louie and the rest of the POWs conspire to kill the Bird by contaminating his rice with infected feces. Four hundred new POWs are marched into Naoetsu from POW camps in larger cities that have been destroyed by U.S. B-29 bombers. They inform Louie that Germany has fallen and Japan remains in the war alone. Fish is stolen from a worksite, and the men get caught. Rather than punish the culprits, the Bird orders each man to punch POW officers in the face. Up to 200 punches land on Louie's face, and his nose is broken.

What's the gist of pages 291–293?

Summary of Pages 294–300

Louie becomes the caretaker of a goat on the brink of death. The goat dies, and the Bird beats Louie. On August 1, a huge U.S. air raid is launched. After the bombing, the bombers drop leaflets warning Japanese civilians of further bombings in Hiroshima and Nagasaki. The Bird tells Louie, "Tomorrow I'm going to drown you" (297), but instead he beats him senseless and leaves him with the threat of drowning him the next day. Again, Louie plots to kill the Bird. On August 6, 1945, the United States drops an atomic bomb on the city of Hiroshima.

What's the gist of pages 301–308?

Summary of Pages 309–329

Five days after the atomic bomb is dropped, the commander of the camp tells Louie and the POWs that "The emperor has brought peace to the world" (309). Days later, American fighter planes drop food supplies to starving POWs. Louie and his fellow POWs celebrate. The Bird escapes. The United States sends planes to transport POWs out of Japan. Louie is flown to Okinawa to recuperate. His family waits anxiously for his return home. Months later, Louie and Pete reunite in San Francisco. The entire family celebrates Louie's return on a runway in Long Beach, California. *(See a picture of this reunion on page 330.)* Phil reunites with his family, marries Cecy immediately, and the two run away to a place where no one can find them. On September 2, 1945, Japan formally surrenders and World War II ends.

Focus Question

Why do the men doubt that the war is over?

EXPEDITIONARY
LEARNING

Vocabulary

Word	Definition	Context clues: How did you figure out this word?
emaciated (291)		
liquidated (292)		
stricken (301)		
innocuous (303)		
inuring (305)		

Being Made Invisible Anchor Chart

Dehumanization		Isolation	
Synonyms and Related Phrases	Examples	Synonyms and Related Phrases	Examples

Invisibility Synonyms Strips

loss of dignity

-----

loss of identity

-----

objectification

-----

exclusion

-----

solitude

-----

separation

-----

loss of community

-----

being "cut off" from others

-----

disconnection

-----

absence

Informational Essay Prompt and Grades 6–8 Expository Writing Evaluation Rubric

Source: Based on a rubric created for the New York State Common Core Curriculum.

Name: _____

Date: _____

During World War II, what were the efforts to make both Japanese-American internees and American POWs in Japan "invisible" and how did each group resist? Use the strongest evidence from *Unbroken* and selected other informational sources about Japanese-American internees.

Criteria	SCORE		
	4 **Essays at This Level:**	**3** **Essays at This Level:**	**This means, in my informational essay, I need to . . .**
CONTENT AND ANALYSIS: the extent to which the essay conveys complex ideas and information clearly and accurately in order to support claims in an analysis of topics or texts	Clearly introduce a topic in a manner that is compelling and follows logically from the task and purpose Demonstrate insightful analysis of the text(s)	Clearly introduce a topic in a manner that follows from the task and purpose Demonstrate grade-appropriate analysis of the text(s)	
COMMAND OF EVIDENCE: the extent to which the essay presents evidence from the provided texts to support analysis and reflection	Develop the topic with relevant, well-chosen facts, definitions, concrete details, quotations, or other information and examples from the text(s) Sustain the use of varied, relevant evidence	Develop the topic with relevant facts, definitions, details, quotations, or other information and examples from the text(s) Sustain the use of relevant evidence, with some lack of variety	

Criteria	SCORE		
	4 Essays at This Level:	3 Essays at This Level:	This means, in my informational essay, I need to . . .
COHERENCE, ORGANIZATION, AND STYLE: the extent to which the essay logically organizes complex ideas, concepts, and information using formal style and precise language	Exhibit clear organization, with the skillful use of appropriate and varied transitions to create a unified whole and enhance meaning Establish and maintain a formal style, using grade-appropriate, stylistically sophisticated language and domain-specific vocabulary with a notable sense of voice Provide a concluding statement or section that is compelling and follows clearly from the topic and information presented	Exhibit clear organization, with the use of appropriate transitions to create a unified whole Establish and maintain a formal style using precise language and domain-specific vocabulary Provide a concluding statement or section that follows from the topic and information presented	
CONTROL OF CONVENTIONS: the extent to which the essay demonstrates command of the conventions of standard English grammar, usage, capitalization, punctuation, and spelling	Demonstrate grade-appropriate command of conventions, with few errors	Demonstrate grade-appropriate command of conventions, with occasional errors that do not hinder comprehension	

EXPEDITIONARY
LEARNING

Rubric Criteria Strips

From "3" Column of the Grades 6–8 Expository Writing Evaluation Rubric

1) Content and Analysis: *"clearly introduce a topic in a manner that follows from the task and purpose"*

This means, in my informational essay, I need to . . .

- -

2) Command of Evidence: *"develop the topic with relevant facts, definitions, details, quotations, or other information and examples from the text(s)"*

This means, in my informational essay, I need to . . .

- -

3) Coherence, Organization, and Style: *"exhibit clear organization, with the use of appropriate transitions to create a unified whole"*

This means, in my informational essay, I need to . . .

----

4) Coherence, Organization, and Style: *"establish and maintain a formal style using precise language and domain-specific vocabulary"*

This means, in my informational essay, I need to . . .

----

5) Coherence, Organization, and Style: *"provide a concluding statement or section that follows from the topic and information presented"*

This means, in my informational essay, I need to . . .

----

6) Control of Conventions: *"demonstrate grade-appropriate command of conventions, with occasional errors that do not hinder comprehension"*

This means, in my informational essay, I need to . . .

---

7) Rubric Criteria Strip for Modeling: *"demonstrate grade-appropriate analysis of the text(s)"*

This means, in my informational essay, I need to . . .

EXPEDITIONARY
LEARNING

Quote Sandwich Guide for Informational Essay

A sandwich is made up of three parts—the bread on top, the filling in the middle, and the bread on the bottom. A "quote sandwich" is similar; it is how you incorporate quotes from texts into an essay. First, you introduce a quote by telling your reader where it came from. Then, you include the quote. Last, you explain how the quote supports your idea.

Introduce the quote.

This includes the "who" and "when" of the quote.

Sample sentence starters for introducing a quote:

In Chapter _____, _____.

When Louie is _____, he_____.

After _____, Miné_____.

Include the quote.

Make sure to punctuate the quotes correctly using quotation marks.

Remember to cite the page number in parentheses after the quote.

Analyze the quote.

This is where you explain how the quote supports your idea.

Sample sentence starters for quote analysis:

This means that _____.

This shows that _____.

This demonstrates that _____.

Informational Essay Planner

Name: _____

Date: _____

Focusing Question

During World War II, what were the efforts to make both Japanese-American internees and American POWs in Japan "invisible," and how did each group resist?

Reminders:

• As you plan your essay, be intentional about writing sentences in the active or passive voice.

• Make sure that your spelling is correct, especially of names, places, and other domain-specific vocabulary.

I. Introduction	
A. Hook to capture the reader's interest and attention	
B. Give brief background information to the reader about the texts (historical context and who Louie and Miné were, etc.)	
C. Topic or focus statement	

II. Body Paragraph 1	
Context for the first reason that supports your focus statement	
A. Topic sentence	
B. Evidence 1	
C. Evidence 2	
D. Evidence 3	
E. Concluding sentence	

III. Body Paragraph 2	
Context for the second reason that supports your focus statement	
A. Topic sentence	
B. Evidence 1	
C. Evidence 2	
D. Evidence 3	
E. Concluding sentence	

IV. Conclusion

A. Restate focus statement	
B. Summarize reasons	
C. What do the experiences of these two people show about the ability of humans to recover, even from deeply difficult experiences?	

End-of-Unit Assessment

Informational Essay Prompt

Name: _____

Date: _____

For the End-of-Unit 2 Assessment, write your best first draft of your informational essay that addresses the prompt:

During World War II, what were the efforts to make both Japanese-American internees and American POWs in Japan "invisible," and how did each group resist? Use the strongest evidence from *Unbroken* and selected other informational sources about Japanese-American internees.

Remember to keep today's learning targets in mind as you write and use the resources you have available, especially your Informational Essay Planner.

Becoming Visible Again Anchor Chart

Name: _____

Date: _____

Dignity		Reconnecting	
Synonyms and Related Phrases	Examples	Synonyms and Related Phrases	Examples

Visibility Synonyms Strips

individuality

---

pride

---

identity

---

self-respect

---

self-esteem

---

self-worth

---

self-control

---

agency

---

involvement

---

presence

----

belonging

----

inclusion

Unbroken Structured Notes

Pages 334–344

Name: _____

Date: _____

What's the gist of pages 334–344?

Summary of Pages 339–344

Louie goes to Miami Beach for two weeks of rest and relaxation. It is there that he meets beautiful, wealthy, pedigreed Cynthia Applewhite. It is love at first sight for Louie. After two weeks of dating, he asks her to marry him. He finishes his speaking tour, and Cynthia flies out to California to meet the family and see him. They marry by the end of May, but not with the full blessing of Cynthia's parents. Louie's drinking is starting to become a problem.

Focus Question

On page 338, Hillenbrand writes, "When the harsh push of memory ran through Louie, reaching for his flask became as easy as slapping a swatter on a fly." What is happening to Louie? Why?

Vocabulary

Word	Definition	Context clues: How did you figure out this word?
corroborated (334)		
intercepted (336)		
whereabouts (336)		
Odyssean (337)		
bewilderment (338)		

EXPEDITIONARY
LEARNING

Sentence Voice and Mood

Name: _____

Date: _____

Active and Passive

What does active voice indicate? _____

What does passive voice indicate? _____

Choose the sentence that helps the reader make meaning best. Explain your choice.

1a. The *Green Hornet* was crashed by a combination of mechanical failure and human error.

1b. A combination of mechanical failure and human error crashed the *Green Hornet*.

Explain:

_____

_____

2a. Sharks attacked the raft when it began to deflate.

2b. The raft was attacked by sharks when it began to deflate.

Explain:

_____

_____

3a. Phil and Louie expected the worst on Kwajalein.

3b. The worst was expected by Phil and Louie on Kwajalein.

Explain:

_____

_____

4a. Dignity was brought to the POWs at Ofuna through small acts of defiance.

4b. Small acts of defiance brought dignity to the POWs at Ofuna.

Explain:

_____

_____

Active and Passive

What is important to remember when using active or passive voice?

_____

_____

Conditional and Subjunctive

What does the conditional mood indicate?

_____

_____

What does the subjunctive mood indicate?

_____

_____

1. If a pilot made a mistake, the plane _____ crash.

   Explain:

   _____

   _____

2. If Louie _____ going to survive, he would need to tap into his "resilient optimism."

   Explain:

   _____

   _____

3. In the POW camps, the conditions were so terrible men _____ die of many preventable diseases.

   Explain:

   _____

   _____

4. The Bird was so unpredictable and violent, he _____ do anything.

   Explain:

   _____

   _____

Conditional and Subjunctive

What is important to remember when using the conditional or subjunctive mood?

_____

_____

Visibility Double Arrow Graphic Organizer

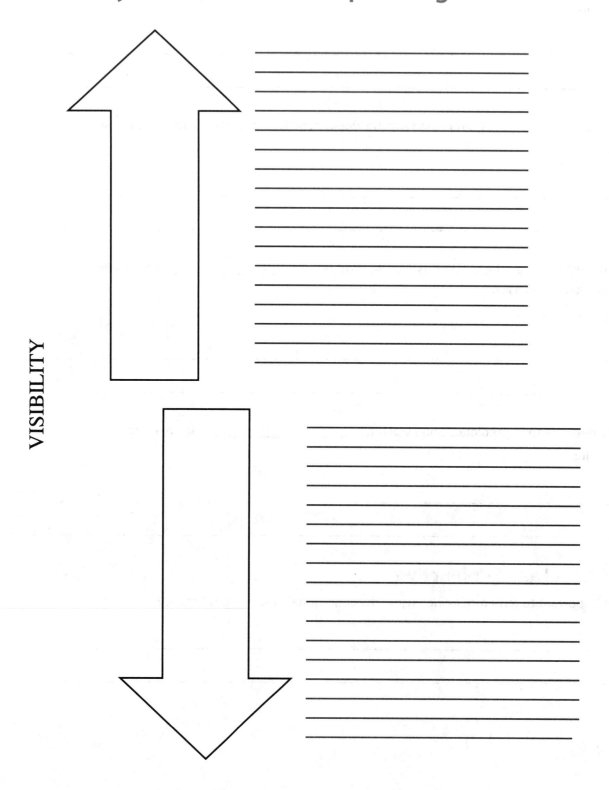

VISIBILITY

Unbroken Structured Notes

Pages 345–353

Name: _____

Date: _____

What's the gist of pages 345–353?

Focus Question

Holocaust survivor Jean Amery described "a seething, purifying thirst for revenge" that some men experienced after being imprisoned in Nazi concentration camps. How is Louie an example of what Amery describes?

Vocabulary

Word	Definition	Context clues: How did you figure out this word?
garrulous (345)		
ravaged (346)		
debilitating (346)		
insidious (346)		
flashbacks (347)		
cogently (348)		

Unbroken Structured Notes

Pages 354–380

Name: _____

Date: _____

What's the gist of pages 354–top of 356?

Summary of Pages 356–361

At the end of the war, more than 5,400 Japanese were tried as war criminals; of those numbers, 4,400 were convicted, 984 were sentenced to death and 475 to life in prison. In Sasaki's trial, it was revealed that he was in truth a low-ranking interpreter, not the high-ranking official he had claimed to be. The Bird had vanished into the mountains, where he became a farmer's assistant and then a waiter. Later he herded cows. In 1946, two bodies were found in the Okuchichibu Mountains. One was identified as the Bird.

What is the gist of what you read on pages 363–376?

What is the gist of what you read on pages 377–380?

Focus Question

On page 365, Hillenbrand writes, "No one could reach Louie because he had never really come home." What finally brings Louie home?

Vocabulary

Word	Definition	Context clues: How did you figure out this word?
incognito (356)		
imperatives (355)		
lucidity (363)		
paradox (366)		
cleave (367)		

Verbals

Name: _____

Date: _____

Verbals: A verbal is a word formed from a verb but functioning as a different part of speech.

A **gerund** is a verbal that ends in -ing and acts as a noun. Examples:

- Nobody appreciates his *singing.*
- *Swimming* is a great sport.

A **participle** is a verbal that most often ends in -ing or -ed and acts as an adjective. Examples:

- My knees *shaking,* I walked into the principal's office.
- The *cracked* windows need to be fixed.

An **infinitive** is a verbal consisting of the word "to" plus a verb and acts as a noun, adjective, or adverb. Examples:

- Now is the best time *to start.*
- My sister agreed *to give* me a ride.

TIP: Don't confuse verbals with verbs. Verbals look like verbs but don't act like verbs.

In each sentence from *Unbroken* below, underline the verbal and identify the type on the line.

1. _____ "The physical injuries were lasting, debilitating, and sometimes deadly" (346).

2. _____ "The central struggle of postwar life was to restore their dignity" (349).

3. _____ "Like many elite athletes, he . . . had never seriously contemplated life after running" (350).

4. _____ "Louie threw himself into training" (350).

5. _____ "His mind began to derail" (352).

6. _____ "One day he opened a newspaper and saw a story that riveted his attention" (352).

Text-Dependent Questions

Becoming Visible Again

Text-dependent questions	Response using the strongest evidence from the text
1. On his first visit to the tent, what did the preacher, Billy Graham, say that affected Louie?	
2. How did Louie react during Graham's sermon? • Why does the author tell us Louie is repeating, "I am a good man"? • What does this have to do with his search for visibility?	
3. What was Graham's message on the second night? • What does Graham mean by "the intangible blessings that give men the strength to outlast their sorrows"?	
4. Why does the author bring us back to the raft? • Why does Louie remember his own gratitude on the raft? • What does the author mean when she says, "The only explanation he could find was one in which the impossible was possible"?	

5. Why does the author end this description with "Louie felt rain falling"? • What was the immediate effect of this moment on Louie?	
6. Looking at the Becoming Visible Again Anchor Chart, what synonyms and examples of dignity now appear to describe Louie?	

Unbroken Structured Notes

Pages 381–389

Name: _____

Date: _____

What's the gist of pages 381–389?

Focus Question

In what ways is Louie's later life still an example of his "resilient optimism"?

Vocabulary

Word	Definition	Context clues: How did you figure out this word?
dilapidation (381)		
ungovernable (381)		
rapt (382)		
improbably (382)		
honoraria (383)		

Verbals II

Name: _____

Date: _____

Remember, a verbal is a word formed from a verb but functioning as a different part of speech in a sentence.

In the chart below, identify the three types of verbal and how each type acts in sentences.

Verbal	Function in sentence

Underline and label the verbals in the examples below.

- "He'd spent two years manning backhoes, upending boulders, and digging a swimming pool" (381).
- "He took the boys fishing, swimming, horseback riding, camping, and in winter, skiing" (381).
- "He made just enough money to keep Cissy and her little brother, Luke, in diapers, then blue jeans, then college" (383).
- "In time even his injured leg healed" (383).
- "Bill Harris ended the war in grand style, plucked from Omori to stand on the *Missouri* as Japan surrendered" (386).
- "At ninety, Pete had the littlest kids in his neighborhood in training" (388).

Unbroken Thematic Statements

Thematic concept: SURVIVAL	Thematic concept: RESILIENCE	Thematic concept: REDEMPTION
What is survival?	What is resilience?	What is redemption?
Where does survival appear in *Unbroken*?	Where does resilience appear in *Unbroken*?	Where does redemption appear in *Unbroken*?

Based on the details above, what is *Unbroken*'s overall message (thematic statement) about survival?	Based on the details above, what is *Unbroken*'s overall message (thematic statement) about resilience?	Based on the details above, what is *Unbroken*'s overall message (thematic statement) about redemption?

Narrative Writing

Becoming Visible Again after Internment

During this module, you have learned that there are important yet divergent experiences in war and conflict. For example, both Louie Zamperini and Miné Okubo were American citizens who lived through World War II. Although their experiences of the war differed, both of their stories are important to study to understand how war and conflict affect individuals and society.

Louie's and Miné's stories also share similarities, such as the thematic concept of **the invisibility of captives during World War II**. You have studied Louie's journey from resisting invisibility as a POW to becoming visible again after the war. Now you are going to write a narrative imagining Miné's journey from resisting invisibility as a Japanese-American internee to becoming visible again.

Writing from Miné Okubo's perspective, tell the story of one moment in her struggle to become visible after leaving the internment camp. Use narrative techniques and incorporate information from sources about Okubo's life to write an original narrative. Answer the question: "How did Okubo become visible after her life in the internment camp?" The narrative must end with the sentence, "I was visible again."

First, you will read an article about Miné Okubo's life to learn more about what happened after she left the internment camp. Then, you will choose one of the following moments to write about:

a.   1944: Walter Cronkite interview

b.   1946: publication of *Citizen 13660*

c.   1981: testimony in front of Congress

d.   1993: first production of *Miné: A Name for Herself*

Luckily, you have an excellent model for using narrative writing to communicate real events: Laura Hillenbrand's *Unbroken*. Hillenbrand wrote about a real person—Louie Zamperini—so her text is nonfiction, but she used narrative techniques to bring the story to life. You will use the same techniques you have analyzed in her writing to make your own narrative engaging.

Narrative Writing Rubric

Becoming Visible Again after Internment

Source: Based on the Grade 6–8 Expository Writing Evaluation Rubric, in turn based on a rubric created for the New York State Common Core Curriculum.

	4	3	2	1	0
Content and Analysis	*Clearly introduce a topic in a manner that is compelling and follows logically from the task and purpose:* • The narrative explicitly builds from informational texts and makes inferences about Okubo's life to creatively imagine her process of becoming "visible" again after internment.	*Clearly introduce a topic in a manner that follows from the task and purpose:* • The narrative builds from informational texts about Okubo's life to describe her process of becoming "visible" again after internment.	*Introduce a topic in a manner that follows generally from the task and purpose:* • The narrative generally builds from informational texts about internment to describe an internee's process of becoming "visible" again, but may not be specific to Okubo's life.	*Introduce a topic in a manner that does not logically follow from the task and purpose:* • The narrative does not follow logically from informational texts about Okubo's life or does not describe her process of becoming "visible" again after internment.	*Demonstrate a lack of comprehension of the text(s) or task:* • The narrative demonstrates a lack of comprehension of the informational texts about Okubo's life or the theme of becoming "visible" again after internment.

	4	3	2	1	0
Cohesion, Organization, and Style	*Exhibit clear organization, with the skillful use of appropriate and varied transitions to create a unified whole and enhance meaning:* • The narrative pace flows smoothly, naturally, and logically from an exposition through several related events. *Establish and maintain a formal style, using grade-appropriate, stylistically sophisticated language and domain-specific vocabulary with a notable sense of voice:* • The narrative consistently and creatively	*Exhibit clear organization, with the use of appropriate transitions to create a unified whole:* • The narrative has a beginning, middle, and end that connect to each other to create a unified story. *Establish and maintain a formal style using precise language and domain-specific vocabulary:* • The narrative consistently employs narrative techniques, such as sensory language, dialogue, and details, to develop experiences and events.	*Exhibit some attempt at organization, with inconsistent use of transitions:* • The narrative has a beginning, middle, and end, but there is no clear connection between sections. *Establish but fail to maintain a formal style, with inconsistent use of language and domain-specific vocabulary:* • The narrative employs some narrative techniques but uses these inconsistently.	*Exhibit little attempt at organization, or attempts to organize are irrelevant to the task:* • The narrative is not logically organized to help show Okubo's process of becoming "visible" again. *Lack a formal style, using language that is imprecise or inappropriate for the text(s) and task:* • The narrative techniques used in the narrative are imprecise or inappropriate for developing Okubo's story.	*Exhibit no evidence of organization:* • The narrative has no evidence of organization. *Use language that is predominantly incoherent or copied directly from the text(s):* • The narrative uses language that is generally incoherent or consists only of quotes from informational texts. *Do not provide a concluding statement or section:* • The narrative does not include a conclusion.

4	3	2	1	0
employs narrative techniques, such as sophisticated sensory language, dialogue, and details, to develop experiences and events. *Provide a concluding statement or section that is compelling and follows clearly from the topic and information presented:* • The narrative's compelling conclusion follows logically from and insightfully reflects on earlier events in the narrative.	*Provide a concluding statement or section that follows from the topic and information presented:* • The narrative's conclusion follows logically from and reflects on earlier events in the narrative.	*Provide a concluding statement or section that follows generally from the topic and information presented:* • The narrative's conclusion follows generally from earlier events in the narrative.	*Provide a concluding statement or section that is illogical or unrelated to the topic and information presented:* • The narrative's conclusion is illogical or irrelevant.	

	4	3	2	1	0
Control of Conventions	*Demonstrate grade-appropriate command of conventions, with few errors:* • Use of capitalization, spelling, and punctuation is grade-appropriate with few errors.	*Demonstrate grade-appropriate command of conventions, with occasional errors that do not hinder comprehension:* • Occasional capitalization, spelling, and punctuation errors do not hinder comprehension.	*Demonstrate emerging command of conventions, with some errors that may hinder comprehension:* • Some capitalization, spelling, and punctuation errors may hinder comprehension.	*Demonstrate a lack of command of conventions, with frequent errors that hinder comprehension:* • Frequent capitalization, spelling, and punctuation errors hinder comprehension.	*Are minimal, making assessment of conventions unreliable:* • Capitalization, spelling, and punctuation errors prevent the reader from understanding the narrative.
Use of Language	*Demonstrate grade-appropriate command of language techniques, with few errors:* • Narrative includes verbs in the active and passive voice and in the conditional and subjunctive moods to achieve	*Demonstrate grade-appropriate command of language techniques, with occasional errors that do not hinder comprehension:* • Narrative includes verbs in the active and passive voice and in the conditional and subjunctive mood to achieve particular effects.	*Demonstrate emerging command of language techniques, with some errors that may hinder comprehension:* • Narrative includes verbs in the active and passive voice and in the conditional and subjunctive	*Demonstrate a lack of command of language techniques:* • Narrative does not demonstrate understanding of how to intentionally use verbs in the active and passive voice and in the conditional and subjunctive moods.	*Are minimal, making assessment of language techniques unreliable:* • Narrative does not include variation in voice and mood.

EXPEDITIONARY LEARNING

4	3	2	1	0
particular effects (emphasizing the actor or the action, expressing uncertainty, or describing a state contrary to fact)	Occasional errors do not hinder comprehension	moods to achieve particular effects. Some errors hinder comprehension.		

- If the student writes only a personal response and makes no reference to the text(s), the response can be scored no higher than a 1.
- Responses totally unrelated to the topic, illegible, incoherent, or blank should be given a 0.
- A response totally copied from the informational text(s) with no original student writing should be scored a 0.

Unbroken Structured Notes

Pages 389–398

Name: _____

Date: _____

What's the gist of pages 389–398?

Focus Question

What statement is Hillenbrand trying to make about resilience? What in the text makes you think this?

Vocabulary

Word	Definition	Context clues: How did you figure out this word?
amnesty (390)		
riled (393)		
reconciliation (394)		
cenotaph (394)		
imperious (396)		

Gathering Textual Evidence

Becoming Visible Again after Internment Note-Catcher

Name: _____

Date: _____

Prompt: Writing from Miné Okubo's perspective, tell the story of **one moment** in her struggle to become visible again after leaving the internment camp. Use narrative techniques and incorporate information from sources about Okubo's life to write an original narrative. Answer the question: "How did Okubo become visible again after her life in the internment camp?" The narrative must end with the sentence, "I was visible again."

Evidence of invisibility during World War II (from "The Life of Miné Okubo")	Evidence of visibility after World War II (from source no.:)	Other interesting details and facts about Okubo's life that I want to remember

Evidence of invisibility during World War II (from "The Life of Miné Okubo")	Evidence of visibility after World War II (from source no.:)	Other interesting details and facts about Okubo's life that I want to remember

"Riverside's Miné Okubo"

Source: Adapted from Mary H. Curtin, "Riverside's Miné Okubo," in George N. Giacoppe, *Splinters-Splinters* (blog), Aug. 27, 2011. Accessed on May 23, 2015, http://splinters-splinters.blogspot.com/2011/08/riversides-mine-okubo.html.

Name: _____

Date: _____

Miné Okusssbo was born in Riverside, California, in a rented house on Eleventh and Kansas Streets, on June 27, 1912. While Miné was growing up, the house was surrounded on three sides by citrus groves. She loved playing in the water of the groves' irrigation ditches, found pollywogs there, and sometimes brought them home in a pail, just to watch them swim. Like many other residents, her parents had crossed an ocean to build a new life.

She was the fourth child of seven. Her father, a scholar of Japanese history and philosophy, named her after the Japanese creation goddess Mine [pronounced mee-neh], a great honor. However, most people in her hometown, unfamiliar with the creation goddess, called her "Minnie."

Miné's parents offered to send her to Japanese language school, but she declined, saying, "I don't need to learn Japanese! I'm an American!" She learned Japanese culture at home anyway. Mama taught her calligraphy, and Father endowed her with the Japanese philosophy of the Four Noble Truths, a guide to **ethics**.[1]

In 1931, Miné enrolled at Riverside Junior College. Richard M. Allman, professor of art, quickly recognized Miss Okubo's potential. She had talent and had learned discipline from her artist mother, who assigned her, early on, to paint a different cat every day, making sure to capture the cat's personality, as well as its shape and color. Dr. Allman encouraged the shy, quiet girl to illustrate for the school's newspaper and become art editor of her class of 1933 yearbook. He said she should also pursue advanced study, preferably at the University of California at Berkeley. Miné didn't know where Berkeley was and didn't think she or her family could afford it. Dr. Allman recommended her anyway; Berkeley accepted her and awarded her a scholarship; and with her part-time jobs, she could afford to study with some of America's finest art teachers.

Miné distinguished herself at Berkeley, but missed Riverside, especially Mama. When Miné felt lonely, she pictured Riverside as she remembered it, then painted what she loved most—a **serene**[2] image of Mama, seated in front of her neighborhood church, Bible in her lap, a cat at her side. That painting, "Mama with Cat," featured in exhibitions, books, and magazines, now rests in a place of honor at the Oakland Museum.

Graduating from Berkeley in 1937 with a master's degree in both art and anthropology, Miné won the prestigious Bertha Taussig Traveling Art Fellowship to study art in Europe. The **frugal**[3] Miss Okubo chose

[1] Ethics: morals; ideas about right and wrong
[2] Serene: calm, peaceful
[3] Frugal: careful with money; not spending too much

to take a freighter across the Atlantic, rather than travel via passenger ship, saying there weren't many passengers on board the freighter, but plenty of grain!

She bought a used bicycle as soon as she got to France, rode it all over Paris, and parked by the Louvre, where she could study original art by the Great Masters. In France, she learned more about art, and she learned about French accent marks. She quickly **appropriated**[4] one for her own name, and from then on, signed her work with an accent mark.

As she traveled throughout Europe, she often packed lunch and art supplies into her bicycle's big basket, pedaled to a place that interested her, and stopped to internalize what she saw. Then she created her own image of the place's meaning, its artistic truth. She traveled in over a dozen different European countries while on fellowship.

By September 1939, however, war was coming to Europe. Friends urged her to go home, where it was safer, but she continued to work, until the day she received a telegram from Riverside, saying Mama was very sick. Miné should return home right away.

She had little money with her in Switzerland, her belongings were back in France, and the Swiss-French border was already sealed. Leaving seemed almost impossible, but her Swiss friends loaned her money to travel, and, somehow, she got back to France and worked her way aboard the last American passenger ship leaving Bordeaux, France. Along with terrified refugees hurrying to leave Europe before bombs started falling, Miné headed home, crossing an Atlantic full of unseen dangers. World War II in Europe was declared while they were still at sea.

Miné made it back to Riverside in time to see her mother alive, but Mama died in 1940. After mourning her mother, Miné looked for work. In response to the Depression, America had implemented a series of federal employment programs. They hired artists. Miné returned to the Bay Area, where people knew her work. She was hired to create murals for luxury liners and frescoes for the military bases Treasure Island and Fort Ord, and to work in conjunction with the great Mexican muralist Diego Rivera, in San Francisco.

Glad to be earning money as an artist on important projects, Miné also was pleased to be sharing an apartment with her younger brother, Toku, now a Berkeley student. It was good to be with family again.

But on December 7, 1941, Japan launched a surprise bomb attack on Pearl Harbor. Many Americans, stunned, no longer trusted anybody of Japanese heritage, even those formerly known personally as good neighbors. War changed everything.

People were edgy. Violence against Asians made headlines. A series of presidential decrees ordered people of Japanese heritage to register, then to settle their affairs and prepare for mandatory evacuation from their homes. They had to dispose of all belongings, pack as if going to camp, and bring only what each could carry. Nobody knew how long they would be away.

Miné and her brother were given three days' notice to report. At their Berkeley assembly center, they were assigned collective family number 13660 and were never again referred to by their given names by officialdom. Under armed guard, with other evacuees, they boarded a bus and were driven over

---

[4] Appropriated: took or used something for one's own purposes

a bridge to San Bruno's former racetrack, Tanforan, now an assembly center, where they lived for six months in a horse stall.

Cameras were forbidden to internees, but Miss Okubo, knowing Americans wouldn't believe what was happening unless they saw it for themselves, determined to document every day she spent behind barbed wire. Carrying her sketch pad throughout the camp, she carefully recorded all she saw and experienced.

After six months at Tanforan, she was shipped to Topaz, an internment camp in the desert of central Utah. Behind another set of barbed wire, she meticulously committed to paper all aspects of internment. She also taught art to interned children and illustrated covers for the three issues of *Trek,* the newsmagazine produced by and for the camp's internees.

From her first week in internment to her last, she kept up extensive correspondence with friends outside. She even entered a Berkeley art contest by mail. She won! That brought her to the attention of the editors of *Fortune* magazine, in New York City, who were planning a special April 1944 issue featuring Japanese culture. They offered Miss Okubo a job, illustrating their special edition. They asked her to please come to New York City within three days.

To leave Topaz, she had to undergo extensive security and loyalty checks. When finally cleared and en route to New York City, she reflected on her years of internment and wondered how she'd be able to adjust to open society again.

Fortune magazine's editors welcomed her, helped her find an apartment, and put her right to work. When they saw her camp drawings, they were so impressed that they dedicated a full-blown illustrated article to internment camps, the first published in a national magazine.

After the special issue came out, the most trusted man in news, Walter Cronkite, gave his entire nationally televised CBS program to his interview with Miss Okubo. The shy girl from Riverside had become a national phenomenon.

Urged to publish her camp drawings as a book, Miné added short captions and called the book *Citizen 13660.* Columbia University Press published it in 1946, to great reviews, after which Miné toured the country, telling her story, exhibiting her art, and making a special stop to see friends at the Riverside Public Library.

She taught art at U.C. Berkeley for two years, then returned to New York to devote herself full time to her own art. Her illustrations appeared in major magazines, newspapers, and scientific books, and her artwork was exhibited from Boston to Tokyo.

In 1981, she testified on behalf of internees at New York City's congressional hearings of the U.S. Commission on Wartime Relocation and Internment of Civilians, presenting the commissioners with a copy of *Citizen 13660.*

Miss Okubo received many honors for her work and her commitment. In 1973, the Oakland Museum hosted a major retrospective of her work; in 1974, Riverside Community College named her Alumna of the Year; in 1987, the California State Department of Education featured her as one of twelve California women pioneers in *The History of California (1800 to Present),* on their large classroom poster, "California Women: Courage, Compassion, Conviction," and in *An Activities Guide for Kindergarten Through Grade 12*; in 1991, she received Washington, D.C.'s National Museum for Women in the Arts' Women's Caucus for Art Honor Award; in 1993, Japan featured her in their 2006 National High School yearbook, used in all Japanese schools; and in the same year, Riverside Community College paid her tribute by renaming a street on campus after her and featuring the original play, *Miné: A Name for Herself,* at their Landis Performing Arts Center. The Smithsonian Institution later selected that play for its 2007 Day of Remembrance and sponsored its performance in Washington, D.C.

Miné Okubo dedicated her life to art. She portrayed truth and beauty with **integrity**,[5] and she did it with such simplicity that a child of seven could appreciate and understand her renderings.

When Miss Okubo died on February 1, 2001, obituaries appeared in newspapers from New York to New Zealand. Memorials were held in New York City, Oakland, and Riverside. She left a legacy of courage, discipline, and love.

Her work continues to enlighten and to challenge. Her artwork hangs in major galleries and is treasured by collectors worldwide; her book, *Citizen 13660,* continues to be studied in classrooms across America and Canada.

[5] Integrity: honesty; with solid principles and beliefs

EXPEDITIONARY
LEARNING

"Miné Okubo"

Source: Adapted from Chelsie Hanstad, Louann Huebsch, Danny Kantar, and Kathryn Siewert, "Miné Okubo," Voices from the Gaps, University of Minnesota, May 3, 2004. Accessed on May 23, 2015, http://voices.cla.umn.edu/artistpages/okuboMine.php.

Name: _____

Date: _____

> In the camps, first at Tanforan and then at Topaz in Utah, I had the opportunity to study the human race from the cradle to the grave, and to see what happens to people when reduced to one status and one condition.
>
> **—Preface to the 1983 edition of *Citizen 13660***

Miné Okubo was born on June 27, 1912, in Riverside, California, to Japanese immigrant parents. From an early age Okubo was interested in art, and her parents always encouraged her to develop her artistic talent. To **refine**[1] her craft, Okubo attended Riverside Community College and, later, the University of California at Berkeley, where she earned a master of fine arts degree. In 1938, Okubo was the recipient of the Bertha Taussig Traveling Art Fellowship, which presented her with the once-in-a-lifetime opportunity to travel to Europe and continue her development as an artist. However, because of the outbreak of World War II and her mother's illness, Okubo was forced to cut her stay in Europe short and return home. Upon her return, Okubo was commissioned by the United States Army to create murals. It was during this time that Okubo's mother passed away.

On December 7, 1941, the Japanese government bombed Pearl Harbor, an event that would forever **alter**[2] Okubo's life as well as the lives of 110,000 other Americans of Japanese descent. On April 24, 1942, she was forced to relocate to the Japanese internment camp of Tanforan. Here, Okubo produced countless paintings and drawings that documented the life of the internees. In 1944, with World War II coming to a close, the editors of *Fortune* relocated Okubo to New York City, where she worked as an illustrator for the magazine. In 1946, Okubo published a book of her paintings, drawings, and sketches from the internment camps, titled *Citizen 13660*.

The dramatic, detailed artistry and brief text depict life in the camps, recording Okubo's observations and experiences. Her pen-and-ink drawings document daily life, and each picture is accompanied by captions that thoroughly explain each scene. Cameras were not allowed inside of these camps, which makes Okubo's artwork even more valuable. *Citizen 13660* helped give voice to the tragic and shameful internment of the Japanese-American community, propelling this disgraceful act onto the center of the American social stage.

[1] Refine: improve
[2] Alter: change

Many critics at the time considered *Citizen 13660* to be a very significant record of the internment of Japanese Americans. American novelist Pearl S. Buck said that, "[Miné Okubo] took her months of life in the concentration camp and made it the material for this amusing, heart-breaking book . . . The moral is never expressed, but the **wry**[3] pictures and the **scanty**[4] words make the reader laugh—and if he is an American too—sometimes blush." The *New York Times Book Review* called *Citizen 13660* "A remarkably objective and **vivid**[5] and even humorous account . . . In dramatic and detailed drawings and brief text, she documents the whole episode—all that she saw, objectively, yet with a warmth of understanding." As a result of the publication of *Citizen 13660*, Okubo was featured on national television when Walter Cronkite interviewed her on his show.

Interest dwindled as years passed, however, and *Citizen 13660* became less important to the American public, including to Japanese Americans. As Okubo herself wrote, "The war was forgotten in the fifties. People throughout the country were busy rebuilding their lives."

As many third-generation Japanese Americans had been very young, or not yet born, during the internment, they first found it hard to grasp its importance. When many of them started attending college in the late 1960s and early 1970s, they began to understand the terrible injustice that had happened to their parents and grandparents. They organized and demanded that people again discuss the internment and that the government give reparations to those who were affected by it. It was this issue that brought about the second publication of *Citizen 13660* in 1973. This reprinting introduced the book to many new readers who not only had never heard of it, but also had never even heard of the internment of Japanese Americans. In 1981, Okubo testified on behalf of all Japanese-American internees at New York City's congressional hearings of the U.S. Commission on Wartime Relocation and Internment of Civilians. She even gave the commissioners a copy of *Citizen 13660*. The University of Washington Press reprinted the book again in 1983.

After publishing *Citizen 13660,* Okubo continued to create numerous artistic works and serve as an important voice for the Japanese-American community. She was honored by receiving several awards and having her artwork exhibited numerous times. A play about her life, titled *Miné: A Name for Herself,* was performed at Riverside Community College in 1993. New York City remained her home until her death at the age of eighty-eight on February 10, 2001.

[3] Wry: amusing in an ironic or unexpected way
[4] Scanty: sparse, little, few
[5] Vivid: bright, lively, clear

Narrative Writing

Becoming Visible Again after Internment Model

Name: _____

Date: _____

I hear the heavy metal gate of the internment camp slam shut behind me, the guard's voice echoing in my ears: "Number 13660: discharged." My identity is a number. My name has been erased. I am invisible. And the Utah desert lies before me, whole and open and terrifying.

I have lived behind the barbed-wire fence of an internment camp for the last two years. My brother, Toku, and I were forced to relocate after the Japanese bombed Pearl Harbor in 1941. Suddenly, we were the enemy, even though we were both born and raised in California. I don't even speak Japanese, but the government was convinced that I was a threat because of my jet-black hair, my Japanese ancestors, my hard-to-pronounce name.

Now, I have been allowed to escape. I am leaving Toku behind to move to New York City. I have been hired as a magazine artist. My drawings of life inside the camp are carefully rolled up inside my bag.

_____

The day before I am scheduled to leave for New York, I travel to Oakland, California. Before I was relocated (that's what they call it, "relocated," although it felt more like being captured and imprisoned), I was hired to create murals for this city. I stalk down one street, peer down another, trying to remember the exact location of one of my murals. I turn a corner and there it is—my art, splashed carelessly across the wall. I was a different person when I made this. I existed. People could see me. Now I am a shadow.

I notice a piece of paint coming loose from the bricks. I pinch it between my fingers and pull. It flakes off and flutters to the ground. The spot of naked brick left behind makes my throat sore and my eyes water.

_____

Every night, I dream that this was all a big mistake. In my dreams, the guards mixed me up with someone else. They come for me here in New York. I dream that the guards climb up the metal fire escape, squeeze through the window, and drag me from my bed. They toss me into a bag and fling me out the window to the street below. I imagine myself screaming, but no one can hear me over the roar of the traffic. In my dreams, everyone on the street is laughing at something I can't see.

Every morning, I wake terrified, as if I've actually been captured. Then I remember that the guards in the camp never touched me. They treated me like I didn't exist. But this doesn't make sleeping any easier.

Yesterday, I walked to the magazine office for the first time, my drawings carefully pressed into a secondhand briefcase they gave me. As I walked, I passed a newsstand filled with magazines and newspapers. I scanned the headlines and saw one that said, "JAP SPY CAPTURED IN NEW YORK." My heart stopped, trying to stay quiet. I felt as if I were watching myself from far, far away. I looked at my feet to make sure they were still on the ground.

A white woman with her baby bumped into my shoulder. I looked up and met her angry, accusatory eyes. "Excuse me," I whispered.

"You people should be ashamed of yourselves," she sneered. I looked around and realized that her face was mirrored all around me—everywhere I looked, there was another pair of angry eyes, another parent gripping a child's hand more tightly. I wondered again if the guards were coming for me.

I realized what those people saw when they looked at me. A "Jap." They didn't see my face. They saw a head of jet-black hair. An enemy. I pulled my jacket more tightly around me and rushed away from the newsstand and the angry woman, her voice playing over and over in my head: *ashamed.*

I have been in New York for almost three months when it happens. I walk past that same newsstand where I first realized how invisible I was. My eyes scan watchfully over the colorful magazine covers and screaming black-and-white newspaper headlines, dreading their accusations.

Then, one magazine's cover story jumps out at me: "INSIDE THE CAMPS." My drawings! I ignore the stares of people around me and grab the magazine off the stand. I flip through it, seeing my own pictures on the pages inside.

I look up to see the man who owns the newsstand burning holes in my face with his angry eyes. I don't blink. I stare back at him. Then I slap my money down on the counter. "These are my drawings," I say to him. "This is MY story."

The imaginary guards who have stalked me through New York melt away. Relief washes over me. Despite the headlines, despite the stares, despite everything, I am an American citizen. I am no longer just Citizen 13660. I am Miné. I am visible again.

Narrative Writing

Becoming Visible Again after Internment Story Map

Name: _____

Date: _____

Climax

Complication

Reflection

Rising Action

Complication

Exposition

Complication

Conclusion

Remember to include:
• Historical context for your narrative • Introduction of your narrator
• Narrator's perspective on internment

Stars and Steps Recording Form

Part A

Partner's Name: _____

Date: _____

1. Read your partner's Narrative Writing: Becoming Visible Again After Internment story map.
2. The rubric says: "The narrative has a **beginning, middle, and end** that **connect to each other** to create a **unified story**." Give your partner one "star" (positive feedback) and one "step" (something to work on) related to this part of the rubric:

	Sentence starters	Your feedback
Star	• Your narrative's [*name part*] is good, because . . . • I like the way you connected [*name parts*], because . . .	
Step	• I wonder if . . . • Have you thought about . . . ? • You might want to . . .	

3. The rubric says: "The narrative's conclusion follows logically from and reflects on earlier events in the narrative." Give your partner one "star" and one "step" related to this part of the rubric:

	Sentence starters	Your feedback
Star	• Your conclusion is logical, because . . . • I like the way you connected the reflection to [*name part*], because . . .	
Step	• I wonder if . . . • Have you thought about . . . ? • You might want to . . .	

Remember: Be kind, specific, and helpful!

Part B

Partner's Name: _____

Date: _____

1. Read your partner's Narrative and Language Techniques: Becoming Visible Again after Internment Planner.

2. The rubric says: "The narrative consistently employs **narrative techniques**, such as sensory language, dialogue, and details, to develop experiences and events." Give your partner one "star" (positive feedback) and one "step" (something to work on) related to this part of the rubric:

	Sentence starters	Your feedback
Star	• The way you used [*technique*] works, because . . . • I like the way you used [*technique*], because . . .	
Step	• I wonder if . . . • Have you thought about . . . ? • You might want to . . .	

3. The rubric says: "Narrative includes verbs in the **active and passive voice** and in the **conditional and subjunctive moods** to achieve particular effects (emphasizing the actor or the action, expressing uncertainty, or describing a state contrary to fact)." Give your partner one "star" and one "step" related to this part of the rubric:

	Sentence starters	Your feedback
Star	• The way you used [*technique*] works, because . . . • I like the way you used [*technique*], because . . .	
Step	• I wonder if . . . • Have you thought about . . . ? • You might want to . . .	

Remember: Be kind, specific, and helpful!

EXPEDITIONARY
LEARNING

Sample Narrative and Language Techniques

Name: _____

Date: _____

1. Read each passage from the model narrative.

2. Label each passage with the name of the narrative or language technique it uses: *pacing, word choice, transition words/phrases, active/passive voice,* or *subjunctive/conditional verb.*

3. Explain the effect of this technique. (In other words, why did the author choose to use this technique here?)

Passage 1: "My brother, Toku, and I were forced to relocate after the Japanese bombed Pearl Harbor in 1941 . . . Now, I have been allowed to escape."	
What narrative or language technique does this passage use?	How does this technique affect the narrative?

Passage 2: "The day before I am scheduled to leave for New York, I travel to Oakland, California . . . I stalk down one street, peer down another, trying to remember the exact location of one of my murals. I turn a corner and there it is—my art, splashed carelessly across the wall."	
What narrative or language technique does this passage use?	How does this technique affect the narrative?

Passage 3: "I notice a piece of paint coming loose from the bricks. I pinch it between my fingers and pull. It flakes off and flutters to the ground. The spot of naked brick left behind makes my throat sore and my eyes water."	
What narrative or language technique does this passage use?	How does this technique affect the narrative?

Passage 4: "Every morning, I wake terrified, as if I've actually been captured."	
What narrative or language technique does this passage use?	How does this technique affect the narrative?

Passage 5: "I have been in New York for almost three months when it happens."	
What narrative or language technique does this passage use?	How does this technique affect the narrative?

Passage 6: "Relocated (that's what they call it, 'relocated,' although it felt more like being captured and imprisoned)."

What narrative or language technique does this passage use?	How does this technique affect the narrative?

Passage 7: "I dream that the guards climb up the metal fire escape, squeeze through the window, and drag me from my bed. They toss me into a bag and fling me out the window to the street below."

What narrative or language technique does this passage use?	How does this technique affect the narrative?

Passage 8: "I looked around and realized that her face was mirrored all around me."	
What narrative or language technique does this passage use?	How does this technique affect the narrative?

Passage 9: "I don't blink. I stare back at him. Then I slap my money down on the counter."	
What narrative or language technique does this passage use?	How does this technique affect the narrative?

Passage 10: "Yesterday, I walked to the magazine office for the first time."	
What narrative or language technique does this passage use?	How does this technique affect the narrative?

EXPEDITIONARY
LEARNING

Narrative and Language Techniques

Becoming Visible Again after Internment Planner

Name: _____

Date: _____

Narrative Technique	Placement	Reasoning
	(Where/how will I use this in my story?)	*(What effect will this narrative technique help me achieve?)*
Pacing		
Word choice (precise words, sensory language, description)		

Transition words and phrases		
Active/passive voice		
Conditional/ subjunctive verbs		

Mid-Unit Assessment

Single-Draft Narrative Prompt

Becoming Visible Again after Internment

Name: _____

Date: _____

Prompt: "Writing from Miné Okubo's perspective, tell the story of one episode in her struggle to become visible again after leaving the internment camp. Use narrative techniques and incorporate information from sources about Okubo's life to write an original narrative to answer the question, 'How did Okubo become visible again after her life in the internment camp?' The narrative must end with the sentence, 'I was visible again.'"

End-of-Unit Assessment

Analysis of Language Techniques

Name: _____

Date: _____

1. In the chart below, identify the function of each type of verbal.

Verbal	Function in sentence
Infinitive	
Gerund	
Participle	

Identify the type of verbal underlined in the sentences below:

2. _____ "He'd spent the previous summer <u>pedaling</u> through villages on a bicycle fitted with a cooler, selling ice cream, envying the children who played around him" (390).

3. _____ "It was Louie, <u>blushing</u> to the roots of his hair" (40).

4. _____ "He had three days <u>to prepare</u> for the final" (33).

5. _____ "The risks of <u>flying</u> were compounded exponentially in combat" (83).

6. _____ "They'd love <u>to work</u> within the camp, he said, making it a better place" (241).

Complete the sentences below with the correct subjunctive or conditional mood. Explain your choice.

7. If Louise _____ to lose hope that Louie was alive, the family might not have made it through the war.

    Explain:

---

8. When the war was over, many POWs thought they _____ easily return to their old lives.

    Explain:

9. If Louie did not give up his quest to kill the Bird, it _____ have ruined his life.

    Explain:

In the sentence pairs below, determine which conveys meaning in the clearest way. Explain why you chose the active or passive voice.

10. a. Louie was loved by Pete.

    b. Pete loved Louie.

    Explain:

11. a. Christianity brought peace to Louie.

b. Louie was brought peace by Christianity.

Explain:

12. a. Louie was overcome with enthusiasm when he saw his former captors.

b. Enthusiasm overcame Louie when he saw his former captors.

Explain:

13. a. Louie devoted his life to helping boys in danger of going to jail.

b. Boys in danger of going to jail were helped by Louie.

Explain:

John Steinbeck Quotation

"A great lasting story is about everyone or it will not last. The strange and foreign is not interesting—only the deeply personal and familiar."

—John Steinbeck, *East of Eden*

Final Performance Task: Narrative Writing

Becoming Visible Again after Internment

(Group Presentation and Reflection)

Name: _____

Date: _____

After having researched Miné Okubo's life after internment, you have written a narrative in which you told the story of how Okubo went from resisting efforts to make her "invisible" during internment to how she became "visible" post-internment. As part of the Final Performance Task, you will share your narrative in a small-group setting with other students. Then you will reflect on the research-based story you have written.

Narrative Share Task Card

Name: _____

Date: _____

1. Number yourselves 1, 2, 3, and 4, starting with the youngest member of your group and working up to the oldest.

2. Number 1 will read his or her narrative aloud first.

3. While Number 1 is reading, Numbers 2, 3, and 4 will be listening for the answers to these questions:

    •   What details show that Miné is "invisible" at the beginning of the narrative? *(everyone gives a different answer)*

    •   What is the moment that Miné "becomes visible again"? *(everyone agrees on one answer)*

    •   What was one moment in this narrative that you could picture in your head? What did the author do to make this scene so vivid? *(everyone gives a different answer)*

4. When Number 1 has finished reading the narrative, Numbers 2, 3, and 4 tell Number 1 the answers to the questions based on what you have just heard in the narrative.

5. As a group, choose one unique, creative short passage from Number 1's narrative (no more than three sentences long) to read aloud to the whole class later.

6. Repeat with Number 2 reading his or her narrative.

7. Repeat with Number 3 reading his or her narrative.

8. Repeat with Number 4 reading his or her narrative.